EXTEND education

ReviseIB

Design Technology

TestPrep: DP Exam Practice Workbook

A note from us at Extend Education

While every effort has been made to provide accurate advice on the assessments for this subject, the only authoritative and definitive source of guidance and information is published in the official subject guide, teacher support materials, specimen papers and associated content published by the IB. Please refer to these documents in the first instance for advice and guidance on your assessments.

Any exam-style questions in this book have been written to help you practise and revise your knowledge and understanding of the content before your exam. Remember that the actual exam questions may not look like this.

Bhakti Mahendra Ahire and Jonathan Guy Kelly

SL & HL
Standard Level & Higher Level

Published by Extend Education Ltd., 42 Lytton Road, Barnet, Hertfordshire, EN5 5BY, United Kingdom

www.extendeducation.com

The right of Bhakti Mahendra Ahire and Jonathan Guy Kelly to be identified as authors of this work has been asserted by them with the Copyright, Designs and Patents Act 1988.

Reviewed by Glyn Bough

Typesetting by York Publishing Solutions Pvt. Ltd., INDIA

Cover photo by dreamnikon, iStock

First published 2019

23 22 21 20 19

10 9 8 7 6 5 4 3 2 1

ISBN 978-1-913121-01-3

Author acknowledgements

Bhakti Mahendra Ahire: Having an idea and turning it into a book is as hard as it sounds. The experience is both internally challenging and rewarding. I especially want to thank my family, my parent's and my friends who stood hard as rock in all my difficult times and allowing me to follow my ambitions throughout my childhood. I dedicate this book to them. Without their support and motivation, this book would not exist. To all the individuals I have had the opportunity to lead, be led by, or watch their leadership from afar. I want to say thank you for being the inspiration and foundation for the success of this book.

I'd really like to thank Sophie Russell for providing me with the opportunity to become the lead author for this book. I appreciate that she believed in me to provide the leadership and knowledge to make this book a reality. Jonathan Kelly, the contributing author is a great person and a scholar; without him, the perfect blend of knowledge and skills that went into authoring this book would not have been possible. I owe a huge thanks to Naomi Rainbow of Extend Education for providing excellent support and advice consistently throughout the writing. I thank each of the publishers, editors, designers and advisers for devoting their time and effort towards this book. I think that it will be a great asset to the students. Thanks for everything, I look forward to writing the second edition soon! I also wish to thank all of our technical reviewers and the publishing team at Extend Education. I am grateful to work with this entire team and hope the community finds the book useful.

Jonathan Kelly: It's been a great privilege and journey to write this book and I extend huge thanks to Extend Education, Sophie Russell and Naomi Rainbow, and their important team of behind-the-scenes editors, etc. for advice, inspiration and trust in us for this much-needed additional textbook. Co-author Bhakti has been an inspiration and joy to work with. As seasoned and passionate designers, authors and teachers, we are pleased to provide you students with a diverse range of contemporary relevant design issues to contemplate, challenge your thinking and at the same time evoke wonder and joy in this far-embracing subject. The SL and HL theory topics, worth 60% of design technology, are totally relevant with so many contemporary issues to grapple, marvel and solve. So credit to IB here, whom I admire tremendously. I'd like to thank my current school Pathways International School Gurgaon, India: Jains family, School Director Captain Bajaj, my school principals whom I teach MYP Design and DP Design – Ms Sangeeta Nag, Ms Dimpu Sharma, Usha – my trusted design team of talented people. Fellow students and those Pathwaysians out in the field...keep innovating, making the world a better place! Professor Patrick and Neil at University of Southern Queensland, Cambridge, Loughborough – friends and family in UK, NZ, S. Korea. Last but not least, Isabella, Beatrice, Young, Nicky, Mum, Dad, and Toby the all-important family dog!

Copyright notice

Other important information

A reminder that Extend Education is not in any way affiliated with the International Baccalaureate.

Many people have worked to create this book. We go through rigorous editorial processes, including separate answers checks and expert reviews of all content. However, we all make mistakes. So if you notice an error in the book, please let us know at info@extendeducation.co.uk so we can make sure it is corrected at the earliest possible opportunity.

If you are an educator with a passion for creating content and would like to write for us, please contact info@extendeducation.co.uk or write to us through the contact form on our website www.extendeducation.co.uk.

CONTENTS

Picture credits
p9: Cochlear implant (Matt Ralph, Flickr.com (cropped)(CC BY 2.0)); p17: Coffee table (adapted from an original photograph by Ergonomidesign, Wikimedia commons (CC BY-SA 3.0)); p23: Photo by Darren Halstead on Unsplash; p26: Office chair (chair bizarre, Flickr.com (CC BY-SA 2.0)), Bar chair (Frank C. Müller, Baden-Baden, Wikimedia commons (CC BY-SA 4.0)); p29: Wearable smartphone (Chris Harrison, Scott Saponas, Desney Tan, Dan Morris - Microsoft Research, Wikipedia (CC BY-SA 3.0)); p32: Phones (Lledorut, Wikimedia commons (CC BY-SA 4.0)), Typewriter (Valeriana Solaris, Flickr.com (CC BY 2.0)); p39: Bottles (Rob Sinclair, Flickr.com (CC BY-SA 2.0)); p41: Fitness bands (Mile Atanasov/Shutterstock.com), Fitness band (rawf8/istockphoto.com); p42: Turtle in net (Doug Helton, NOAA/NOS/ORR/ERD), Bird in plastic (www.niederrhein-foto.de | Uwe Schmid Wikimedia commons (CC BY-SA 4.0)); p43: Bird in pollution (U.S. Fish and Wildlife Service Headquarters, Flickr.com (CC BY 2.0)), Bottles on beach (wattanaphob, istockphoto.com), Sneakers (Sablin, istockphoto.com); p46: Cockpit (Ralf Roletschek/roletschek.at, Wikimedia commons (CC BY-SA 2.5)); p47: Technical drawing (Emok, Wikimedia commons (CC BY-SA 3.0)), Drill (Pixabay.com); p48: Radio (Antonio-BanderAS/istockphoto.com); p50: Plastic blocks (Moussa81/istockphoto.com); p51: Glass façade (MichaelGaida, Pixabay.com); p52: Hardwood boat (vannino, Pixabay.com), Manufacturing line (Siyuwj, Wikimedia commons (CC BY-SA 3.0)); p53: Smart watch (scanrail/istockphoto.com); p54: Cricket bat and ball (BrianA Jackson/istockphoto.com); p56: Plug (Evan-Amos, Wikimedia commons); p57: Blood collection tube (Myriams-Fotos, Pixabay.com); p58: Seatbelt (M.M.Minderhoud, Wikimedia commons (CC BY-SA 3.0)), Skin-cleansing brush (stux, Pixabay.com); p61: Scooters (Supertrooper/Shutterstock.com); p62: Glass packaging (choness/istockphoto.com); p63: Dark guitar (Chromakey/Shutterstock.com), Light guitar (rosarioscalia/Shutterstock.com); p64: Toddler car (pixabay.com); p66: Dolls (Alexas_Fotos, Pixabay.com); p68: Volvo-7900-Electric-Concept-Bus-UITP-Milan-P1350601" by citytransportinfo is licensed under CC0 1.0; p71: Vedel chair (Gisle Hannemyr/Wikimedia commons (CC BY-SA 2.5)), Vedel chairs (Bukowskis); p75: Shutterstock By Gorlov Alexander; p77: White pulse oximeter (園野, Flickr.com (CC BY-SA 2.0)), black pulse oximeter (Nina Childish, Flickr.com (CC BY-ND 2.0)); p89: Smartphone with stylus (dimarik/istockphoto.com); p93: (c) Hyundai; p95: Wingsuit photograph (SindreEspejord/istockphoto.com), Wingsuit drawings (alongzo/Shutterstock.com); p98: Phone booth (MartinLisner/istockphoto.com); p100: TAP keyboard/mouse (Tap Systems, Inc.); p102: Yamaha Niken by desmodex is licensed under CC BY-SA 2.0; p103: Audi Pop.Up Next at the Geneva Motor Show 2018, Norbert Aepli, Switzerland (CC BY 4.0)

HOW TO USE THIS BOOK

This excellent exam practice workbook has been designed to help you prepare for you design technology exam! It's been divided into the following easy-to-understand sections.

EXPLAIN

The EXPLAIN section gives you a rundown of your paper, including number of marks available, how much time you'll have and the assessment objectives (AOs) and command terms. There's also a handy checklist of your topics you can use as a revision checklist.

SHOW

The SHOW section has some example questions with model student answers so you can see what's expected of you when you answer your own questions in the exam.

TEST

This is your chance to try out what you've learned. The TEST section has full sets of exam-style practice papers filled with the same type and number of questions that you can expect to see in the exam.

Set A Paper 1 (SL)(HL), Paper 2 (SL&HL) and Paper 3 (HL)	Set B Paper 1 (SL)(HL), Paper 2 (SL&HL) and Paper 3 (HL)	Set C Paper 1 (SL)(HL), Paper 2 (SL&HL) and Paper 3 (HL)
Presented with a lot of tips and guidance to help you to get to the correct answer and boost your confidence.	Presented with fewer helpful suggestions and hints so you need to make sure you have revised enough before attempting these papers.	Presented with space to add your own notes and no guidance – the perfect way to test if you are exam ready.
Use these papers early on in your revision...		Use this paper closer to the exam...

Take a look at some of the helpful features in these books that will help guide you in the right direction.

ANSWER ANALYSIS

These boxes include advice on how to get the most possible marks for your answer.

These are general hints for answering the questions.

These flag up common or easy-to-make mistakes that might cost you marks.

This box reminds you of the Assessment Objective being tested.

COMMAND TERMS

These boxes outline what the command term is asking you to do.

These show you when the questions have other interdisciplinary links.

KNOWING YOUR PAPER

In order to achieve higher grades, you need to approach this subject with an inquisitive mind. Make good use of design-related resources and nurture a technological awareness. Before beginning revision, it is always worth taking time to understand what you are expected to do in the exam.

> Make sure that you know exactly what to expect on the day of the exam.

How are you assessed?

You will sit **two** written papers for your exam at the Standard Level, and **three** written papers at the Higher Level.

<table>
<tr><td rowspan="5">Paper 1</td><td>SL</td><td>HL</td></tr>
<tr><td>30 multiple-choice questions based on the core material</td><td>40 multiple-choice questions based on the core material</td></tr>
<tr><td>30% overall grade</td><td>20% overall grade</td></tr>
<tr><td>30 marks</td><td>40 marks</td></tr>
<tr><td>45 minutes</td><td>1 hour</td></tr>
</table>

> Questions in the exam will mostly test your knowledge and the ability to apply design and technology in various interdisciplinary applications.

<table>
<tr><td rowspan="5">Paper 2</td><td>SL*</td><td>HL*</td></tr>
<tr><td colspan="2">Section A – One data-based question and several short answer questions on the core material. (All questions are compulsory)

Section B – One extended response to question on the core material (from a choice of three questions)</td></tr>
<tr><td>30% overall grade</td><td>20% overall grade</td></tr>
<tr><td>50 marks</td><td>50 marks</td></tr>
<tr><td>1 hour 30 minutes</td><td>1 hour 30 minutes</td></tr>
</table>

*This paper is the same for SL and HL

> Practising data-based questions and case studies will help you in improving your analysing and evaluation skills.

<table>
<tr><td rowspan="4">Paper 3</td><td>HL</td></tr>
<tr><td>Section A – Two structured questions on the HL content (both compulsory; each worth 10 marks)

Section B – One structured question based on the HL content based on a case study. (Maximum marks 20)</td></tr>
<tr><td>20% overall grade</td></tr>
<tr><td>40 marks</td></tr>
<tr><td>1 hour 30 minutes</td></tr>
</table>

> The exam questions in design technology will examine your understandings of the social, moral and economic effects of a product or technology on the environment and society.

> The extended response section in the exam paper requires you to construct, analyse and evaluate the technical data given in the case study.

Your assessment objectives

There are **four** assessment objects for design technology (DT). Make sure you are clear on what you need to demonstrate for each one.

Assessment objective	Types of command terms	Which questions test this?	Example questions
Assessment objective 1	Define, Draw, Find, Label, List, Measure, Present, State	Questions in the exam that test your understanding of AO1 are generally worth fewer marks. You will be expected to define, list or state any fact, concept, principle or terminology.	Define the term 'renewable resource'. **[1 mark]**

Assessment objective	Types of command terms	Which questions test this?	Example questions
Assessment objective 2	Annotate, Apply, Calculate, Describe, Distinguish, Estimate, Identify, Outline	Questions in the exam that test your understanding of AO2 are generally expecting you to apply and use the knowledge and practical approach to design technology.	Describe how the characteristics of the parabolic solar cooker are consistent with sustainable development. **[4 marks]**
Assessment objective 3	Analyse, Comment, Compare, Compare and Contrast, Construct, Deduce, Demonstrate, Derive, Discuss, Design, Determine, Evaluate, Discuss, Predict, Explain, Justify, Show or Sketch	Questions in the exam that test your understanding of AO3 are generally expecting you to construct or analyse a design context, process, design technique, design element or a product.	Discuss a design context in which user-centred design is particularly applicable. **[6 marks]**
Assessment objective 4	This AO is assessed in your Internal Assessment, which is worth 40% and consists of one design project. This AO is tested on the performance of the four common assessment criteria of SL and HL, and two additional assessment criteria for HL. This involves the demonstration of proper research, investigation, modelling and personal skills like communication and decision making.		

Before you begin your exam

You should have substantial factual and conceptual knowledge of the following core topics before you take your exams.

Put a tick in each box when you are happy that you have fully studied that topic and are 100% confident with the definitions and interpretations.

Standard level topic checklist

Topic	Studied	Definitions	Case studies	Terminologies	MCQs
1. Human factors and ergonomics	☐	☐	☐	☐	☐
2. Resource management and sustainable production	☐	☐	☐	☐	☐
3. Modelling	☐	☐	☐	☐	☐
4. Final production	☐	☐	☐	☐	☐
5. Innovation and design	☐	☐	☐	☐	☐
6. Classic design	☐	☐	☐	☐	☐

Check you would be able to recognize which section a particular topic or question relates to.

Higher level topic checklist

Additional HL topics	Studied	Definitions	Case studies	Terminologies	MCQs
7. User-centred design	☐	☐	☐	☐	☐
8. Sustainability	☐	☐	☐	☐	☐
9. Innovation and markets	☐	☐	☐	☐	☐
10. Commercial production	☐	☐	☐	☐	☐

Make sure while revising you make use of flowcharts and diagrams as frequently as possible. This will help you to visually recall information for an answer during the exam.

What to do in your exam

Write your candidate session number on the exam paper.

Read all questions carefully before beginning and plan how much time to allocate to each.

Start answering those questions that you feel most confident in. There is no need to answer in order.

If your brain freezes, don't panic. Take a sip of water and just keep writing and you will soon remember more details.

Don't spend more time than you planned on a particular question – you might run out of time!

At the end of your exam, revisit the questions that you were unsure about.

Use every minute left to review your answers before handing over the paper.

ANSWER ANALYSIS

While preparing for the exams, have a look at the previous question paper mark schemes. They will give you an idea of the key points and guidelines that the examiner uses whilst marking.

SHOWING WHAT YOU KNOW

This section of the book can help you to produce better answers to hit the top marks in your exam. Before looking at the example answers, try answering the exam-style questions by yourself first. Then compare your answers with the answers given. Check to see if there are places where you could have communicated more effectively or used more appropriate language and terms.

Paper 1

1. Figure 1 is a bell-shaped curve showing a normal distribution.

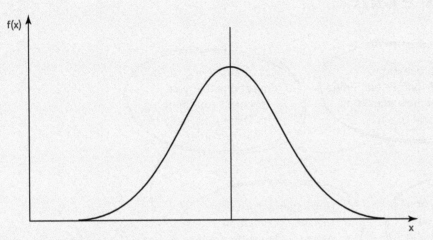

f(x)

x

Figure 1: A bell-shaped curve

Which percentile range should the designer use for a mass-produced product?

☐ A. 1st–99th percentile

☐ B. 95th percentile

☐ C. 50th percentile

☐ D. 5th–95th percentile   [1]

Answer: D

2. What is circular economy?

☐ A. The economy of the country

☐ B. An unsustainable economy

☐ C. A method of securing sustainable practice

☐ D. An economy based on the make, use, dispose model

Answer: C

ANSWER ANALYSIS

In order to get the answer right, you need to read the question carefully: it is asking for the percentile range for a mass-produced product. Option D (5th–95th percentile) provides the best coverage range as there is an inclusion of almost everyone in the design context and only excludes the extremes. Option C (50th percentile) is the most likely or average population (called the mean in statistics) and could be considered for mass production. However, it is not the best answer.

Remember circular economy is aimed at minimizing waste and making the most of the resources.

1. A case study on cochlear implants.

Figure 2: A cochlear implant system

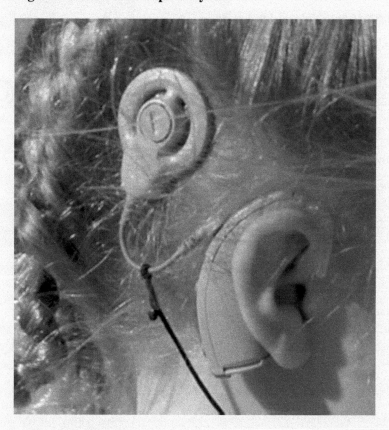

The cochlear implant is a medical aid that is implanted behind the ear of a deaf person. It is used with a microphone and a speech processor that electronically stimulates the auditory nerve and results in the individual being able to hear sound.

When the device was first developed in 1978 by Graeme Clark, it was referred to as the bionic ear. Since then a variety of cochlear implants have been created by the Cochlear division of Nucleus. The implants are designed to be used by both adults and children who can hear very little and receive no benefit from existing hearing aids. The system enables impaired people to perceive most environmental sounds and speeches.

The implant is handcrafted under a microscope and is guaranteed for ten years, but designed for a life of 70 years. The number of Nucleus® implant recipients has grown to over 27,000 globally, with more than 13,000 of these being children. The cochlear implant is an example of innovations in design, combined with engineering, information processing and software design and development.

Define innovation. [2]

Innovation means to commercialize an invention successfully in a marketplace. An invention that is not commercially feasible cannot be considered as an innovation.

> Learn the material with the exam format in mind. Find out as much information as possible about the exam so you can plan your studying accordingly.

> Highlight the key words from the text provided in the question. This can help you to emphasize on key points while writing.

> It is important to remember to read all the information provided in a question carefully as it will give you clues to help answer the questions.

> Make sure you have a good understanding of key terminology by using the IB DP design technology glossary of terms published by the IB (and available online). You are likely to be asked to define specific terms in your exam.

> With 2-mark questions remember not to go into too much detail. Only a couple of sentences will be required.

2. Discuss the reasons for the successful innovation of the cochlear implant in the healthcare industry. What is the role of the designer in making the product viable? **[4]**

Invention and innovation are always a result of a need to solve or simplify a problem. When the innovative idea helps to simplify the problem then the innovation becomes successful. Hence an innovation requires the designer to address the current trends in the market and identify the needs of the users with an existing product. The outcome of understanding the user views is improved usability, better quality and user-friendliness. Designers need to be creative/innovative and firmly grounded in factual and procedural knowledge whilst remembering the needs and limitations of the end users.

This question is asking for two perspectives, one from the market point of view and the second from the designer's point of view. Answer this question while making connections with both perspectives.

ANSWER ANALYSIS

To analyse a product, make sure you maintain an unbiased view and evaluate the context objectively, highlighting its strengths, weaknesses and opportunities.

3. Design is a multidisciplinary approach, from the design and development to the rigorous assessments in the product evaluation. Explain how anthropologists, engineers and psychologists might contribute to the design of Figure 2. **[9]**

Anthropologists

• Anthropologists are involved in the study of characteristics of humans and society as a whole. They are important in this context so the design team can understand and predict people's sociocultural and economic behaviour.

• The research of anthropologists can help the design team to anticipate the people's acceptance or reaction towards the cochlear implant.

• Anthropologists can identify business and user problems and offer solutions based on their analysis and context studies.

Engineers

• Can create concept models of the cochlear implant for evaluation.

• Can create interactive prototypes to test with the market.

• Can build the working implant.

• Can identify and modify hardware and software problems in the implant.

Psychologists

• Can contribute to identifying user personas and scenarios.

• Will have insight that will support the patient and family.

ANSWER ANALYSIS

To answer this type of question correctly it is important to have studied the multidisciplinary approach to innovation. This is possible only if you have up-to-date knowledge of all the topics required for the exam.

ANSWER ANALYSIS

You do not need to write an introduction or conclusion for a 9-mark answer. Organize your answer under the **three** headings covering the three parts of the question (anthropologists, engineers and psychologists). Write three distinct points under each heading to get the full 9 marks.

- Can measure the end-users psychological and physiological experience and discover any problems.
- Can advise on how the implant performs against usability requirements from a psychological perspective.
- Can share their evaluations which are then fed back into the design cycle.

4. List any three types of innovations. **[3]**
   - Sustaining innovation
   - Disruptive innovation
   - Process innovation

5. Successful innovations typically start with detailed design and marketing specifications. Explain the information that can be gathered in a marketing specification in order to create an innovative solution to a product. **[6]**

Design and marketing specifications include information about the target market, which is a specific, well-defined group of consumers that a designer, innovator or a manufacturer aims its products or services at. For example, IKEA is a furniture-manufacturing company whose potential consumers include diverse fields such as educational, household and offices.

A target audience is a demographic group of people likely to be interested in a product or service. For example, a plumbing company's target audience is property owners (commercial and residential) while a toy store's target audience is parents, grandparents, and anyone with children.

Market analysis includes examining existing market products through research and development. A manufacturer needs to understand the expectations and requirements of the users. It also looks at the competition to identify the competitors in the target market.

> Do not repeat the same point in an answer to a 9-mark question. You will lose out on a mark.

> Other possible answers are architectural or configurational innovation and radical innovation. But you won't get more points for naming more than three.

> This question tests AO1 as it expects you to 'list' the specifications, which means you need to give a structure of brief answers with no detailed explanation.

> **ANSWER ANALYSIS**
> In this answer, [1] mark would be awarded for each point made by the student and [1] mark for a correct explanation of that point.

> These types of question have similarities with the focus and objective of Unit 4: Marketing in Business management.

TESTING WHAT YOU KNOW

Set A

Paper 1: Standard Level

Set your timer to 45 minutes.

This paper is worth 30 marks.

Answer **all** the questions in this paper.
For each question, choose the answer you think fits the best.

1. What does using eco-friendly sustainable materials mean that the materials are?
   - ☐ A. Perishable and affordable
   - ☐ B. Easy for replacing and repairing
   - ☐ C. Reusable or recyclable
   - ☐ D. Easily renewable and replaceable   [1]

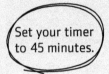 **Eco-friendly**: minimises damage to the environment.

2. Inbuilt obsolescence is a concept adopted by most manufacturing companies into their products. What could be a reason for its adoption?
   - ☐ A. To increase the stability of sales for the manufacturing company
   - ☐ B. To extend the warranty period of the product
   - ☐ C. To make the product environmentally safe after the extended period of time
   - ☐ D. To ensure that the product is always present in the market place   [1]

An example of inbuilt obsolescence could be limiting the lifespan of a light bulb.

Reasons for obsolescence can be due to style, function and technology.

3. Which factor is most important for a designer while considering the design brief for a client?
   - ☐ A. Creating a formal detailed presentation for the audience
   - ☐ B. The overall cost of the research and development of the prototype
   - ☐ C. Making ideas clear for the target audience
   - ☐ D. Making ideas effective for the audience   [1]

A design brief is also known as a design goal.

4. Every design project is unique. What is most likely to cause a delay?
   - ☐ A. Poor organisation in the team
   - ☐ B. Lack of resources in the design laboratory
   - ☐ C. Lack of finances for the project
   - ☐ D. Poor planning in executing the project   [1]

5. What do patents protect the designer's work from?
   - ☐ A. Others trying to authorize, promote and sell off their designs
   - ☐ B. The effective international promotion of their designs
   - ☐ C. Potential marketing controls of the designs
   - ☐ D. The secured production of their design work   [1]

 SL Paper 1 is made up of multiple-choice questions that test knowledge of the core material only.

6. A design team is conducting research on reducing the energy consumption of a manufacturing plant. What should be the first step in their research process?

☐ A. Obtaining overall information on the cost of the energy of the plant

☐ B. Conducting detailed research into the manufacturing plant including the amount and timing of the energy consumption

☐ C. Exploring sustainable resources for the development of user-friendly devices

☐ D. Exchange electricity-consuming devices for battery-operated devices **[1]**

7. A food and beverage company has designed a new logo. What must they do to protect their design from being copied?

☐ A. File a patent of the new logo

☐ B. File a licence agreement for the new logo

☐ C. File a trademark of the new logo

☐ D. File copyright of the new logo **[1]**

8. A toy is being designed for a toddler. What is the most important factor for consideration?

☐ A. Safety

☐ B. Aesthetics

☐ C. Ergonomics

☐ D. Obsolescence **[1]**

9. What do you call the property of a material that enables it to remain functional in its environment?

☐ A. Durability

☐ B. Sustainability

☐ C. Hardness

☐ D. Stiffness **[1]**

10. A prototype is lacking expectations set by the client. What should the designer have done initially to prevent this from happening?

☐ A. Lead better market research for the product

☐ B. Discuss additional sketches of the prototype with the client

☐ C. Conduct a detailed analysis of the product requirements

☐ D. Design an appropriate financial plan for the product **[1]**

11. Which strategy is best suited for a manufacturer to decrease the environmental impact of the washing machine it produces?

☐ A. Reinforce the plastic parts with metal wherever possible in the washing machine

☐ B. Recondition the washing machine by replacing it with newer technologies

☐ C. Increase the capacity of the washing bowl

☐ D. Reduce the power and water usage requirements of the washing machine **[1]**

12. What is life-cycle analysis (LCA) used for?

☐ A. To calculate the product's life at a different stage

☐ B. To evaluate the ecological effects that it causes at various stages of its product's life cycle

☐ C. To compare and evaluate similar sustainable products in the market

☐ D. To define the sustainability of a product after it has been manufactured **[1]**

ANSWER ANALYSIS

Technology and design is constantly changing so it is important to keep up to date in your studies.

A licence agreement is a business contract that allows someone to use a patented good or service.

Make sure you read every choice carefully.

Don't be afraid to research terms you are unsure of. Practising papers will help you to identify the topics that need attention.

ANSWER ANALYSIS

You can select the best answer by using the process of elimination. In this method, mark all the answers that you know are inappropriate and then focus on the remaining answers.

Recondition means to replace or repair.

Calculators are not allowed but you might be expected to carry out simple calculations.

The key stages to a product's life cycle are Launch, Growth, Maturity and Decline.

13. What does a product requirement first require?

   ☐ A. Making a prototype

   ☐ B. Developing an action plan for the design project

   ☐ C. Conducting product evaluation

   ☐ D. Establishing a focus group for the product research   **[1]**

> Don't ignore the word 'first' in the question.

14. What must a product do in order to be successful?

   ☐ A. Meet the user needs and requirements

   ☐ B. Comply with international design standards

   ☐ C. Give a lifetime warranty to its consumers

   ☐ D. Be designed with built-in obsolescence   **[1]**

> Watch out for distracting answers, which are only partly correct.

15. A logo design company has undertaken a new design project. Which of the following is required to happen?

   ☐ A. Every design task is assigned separately to all group members

   ☐ B. Multitasking is required between all the team members involved in the project

   ☐ C. Team members work together to discuss and share their ideas

   ☐ D. A project leader leads the development of all the design ideas in the project   **[1]**

> One of the best ways to revise is to note and reflect on errors you have made in previous exams.

16. What is an important consideration when selecting a sustainable material for a product?

   ☐ A. The durability of the selected material

   ☐ B. The ability of the material to remain stiff in all working conditions

   ☐ C. The material's ability to be renewed

   ☐ D. The cost of the selected material   **[1]**

> A single word in the question can change what the correct answer will be. Here the word 'sustainable' is important.

17. What best describes an entrepreneurial activity?

   ☐ A. It offers financial assistance in the development of the new product

   ☐ B. It undertakes the accountability, vision and monetary support for a new product

   ☐ C. It provides technical support for the new product

   ☐ D. It takes charge of all the social aspects of the new product   **[1]**

> Think about what it means to be an entrepreneur.

18. A furniture designer is developing a study table for school children. What is the factor that they should consider first in the development?

   ☐ A. The needs of the school students

   ☐ B. The material for the study table

   ☐ C. The time required for the completion of the table

   ☐ D. The cost price of the table   **[1]**

> These are all important considerations, but the question has asked for the 'first' one.

19. A novel harvesting tool which helps farmers to sow seeds has been designed. Some of the initial sketches are created by the company. How can they protect their ideas from being exposed in the market?

   ☐ A. Register for a patent

   ☐ B. Contact the international copyright office

   ☐ C. Trademark the name

   ☐ D. Record the business idea   **[1]**

> Use correct logic and reasoning to apply your understanding to different design situations.

> This question is about protecting a company's design, not their name.

20. What defines a designer's ethical approach to designing a product?

□ A. Making products that meet a niche market

□ B. Studying ways to protect the designer's work

□ C. Designing products that avoid the unnecessary consumption of natural resources

□ D. Increasing market sales of the product **[1]**

> If something is niche, it means it is small and specialised.

> Try to answer the question before you see the answers.

21. A working prototype is created. At which stage of the design cycle will it be useful to communicate the solution?

□ A. In understanding the aesthetics of the product for the designer

□ B. In investigating glitches in the manufacturing

□ C. When showing the final design to the focus group

□ D. In developing the preliminary solutions within the design team **[1]**

> Aesthetics refers to the visual attractiveness of a product. This may include shape, form, colour, texture, symmetry and proportion.

22. What describes the characteristics of a product being ergonomic?

□ A. It is in good shape and fit

□ B. It needs the least force in operation

□ C. It is comfortable in functionality and usage

□ D. It uses suitable design standards **[1]**

> Ergonomics is the study of people and their relationship with the environment around them. It is used to design products which are comfortable to use and improve productivity.

23. A student is currently working on a design project. What is most important for them to complete the project successfully?

□ A. An action plan and time management for the project

□ B. Ideation in developing creative and innovative concepts

□ C. Sustainability and selection of materials

□ D. Investigation and improvement of practical skills **[1]**

24. What does appropriate research and development in a product highly rely on?

□ A. Choosing a proper design for the manufacturing process

□ B. Meeting ongoing valuation and feedback

□ C. The capability of designers to evolve original ideas

□ D. A capacity of the company to manage economic issues **[1]**

> Study the research methods, which are literature research, qualitative research and quantitative research.

25. In the design process, after developing the initial design concept, what should a designer do next?

□ A. Collect a good market study

□ B. Decide the manufacturing techniques

□ C. Develop a technical drawing

□ D. Develop further feasible design solutions **[1]**

> Review the product designing process (design cycle). It is present in your IB Design guide.

26. Considering the issues of the industrial waste generated and the emergence of clean technologies as a radical or incremental development, what can designers do to address production waste?

□ A. Reduce the price by using cheaper materials

□ B. Design products with parts that are easy to assemble and replace

□ C. Constrain the functionality of existing products

□ D. Redesign existing products to uphold the market share **[1]**

> Circular economy includes cradle-to-cradle, design for disassembly and design inspired by nature.

27. Why is it vital to develop an operational prototype?

☐ A. To define aesthetic essentials of the product

☐ B. To check the operational and functional qualities of the product

☐ C. To create an ideal fit for promotion on social media

☐ D. To help the company develop a suitable manufacturing process **[1]**

28. What are the prime concerns in designing products that meet the requirements of society?

☐ A. The specific needs and wants of the individuals

☐ B. Ecological effects and beliefs

☐ C. Social trends and expectancies

☐ D. Traditional expectations and opinions **[1]**

29. Conceptual modelling is the starting point to solve a problem from an idea developed in the mind. What is its advantage in comparison to a virtually generated sketch?

☐ A. It offers good accuracy

☐ B. It offers more visually appealing options

☐ C. It is more competent for generating large-scale sketches

☐ D. It is more suitable in conveying early ideas **[1]**

30. What is the most likely reason for designers and manufacturers to use environmentally friendly resources?

☐ A. Safeguarding reserves for future use

☐ B. Increasing ecological mindfulness

☐ C. Safeguarding the use of reused materials

☐ D. Improving the quality of the ecosystem **[1]**

> If you find certain topics difficult try organizing the theories or concepts another way, such as with mind maps, comparison charts, flow charts or numbered lists.

> Don't just choose a good feature of conceptual modelling. The question wants an advantage compared to a virtually generated sketch.

> Check you have answered every question – even if you have to guess. Never leave a multiple-choice question blank.

Paper 1: Higher Level

Set your timer to 1 hour.

This paper is worth 40 marks.

Answer **all** the questions in this paper.
For each question, choose the answer you think fits the best.

1. A designer has been contracted to design the layout of a kindergarten school. Which of the following is the most appropriate method to communicate their initial design ideas to the client?

   ☐ A. A technical drawing

   ☐ B. A functional prototype

   ☐ C. A design report

   ☐ D. A conceptual sketch **[1]**

   > At HL you study some additional topics and sit an extra paper. Paper 1 tests the core topics as well as the additional topics, while Paper 3 only tests the additional topics. Both papers are worth 40 marks.

2. An architect has designed a coffee table (Figure 1) for a corporate office. The coffee table has a touchscreen laptop built into it. Which of the following factors has influenced the architecture's design?

   Figure 1: Coffee table

   > Make sure you read the whole question before selecting an answer.

   ☐ A. Social

   ☐ B. Emotional

   ☐ C. Safety

   ☐ D. Environmental **[1]**

   > MCQs might look as though they seek a straightforward answer but the distractors (the incorrect options) can sometimes be similar to the correct answer to test whether you notice the difference.

3. A designer has been contracted to model a new snack food vending machine and needs to identify suitable materials for the packaging of the snack food. How do they evaluate the appropriate materials for the packaging?

   ☐ A. Make a functional model to test its operation

   ☐ B. Take subject matter experts' advice on the recommended materials

   ☐ C. Test materials with different properties and trial them in similar contexts

   ☐ D. Involve focus groups to receive meaningful feedback on the materials **[1]**

   > A subject matter expert has a deep understanding of a particular subject, process, function, technology, machine or material.

   > A focus group is a market research method for the design team to receive customer-like feedback on a product or service.

4. A design team is multidisciplinary. What produces the best outcome?

☐ A. When there is direct competition between members of the team

☐ B. When members work independently towards a design goal

☐ C. When work is shared between individuals based on their expertise

☐ D. When the workflow is structured correctly **[1]**

5. What is the reason for a product being obsolete?

☐ A. When the product's functionality is improved with only a few modifications to the old design

☐ B. When an innovative design feature is incorporated

☐ C. When the sales of the product decrease

☐ D. When the product has been replaced by a new design **[1]**

6. What is the benefit of making a prototype before starting construction of the model?

☐ A. Permits more efficient teamwork

☐ B. Reduces manufacturing risks

☐ C. Encourages more scope for testing

☐ D. Increases sales in the market **[1]**

7. A design team is about to start developing a new range of products. Part of this process is the implementation of management plans. What do these plans ensure about the product?

☐ A. That it meets the intended purpose

☐ B. Addresses all legal requirements

☐ C. Is developed on time and on budget

☐ D. Meets the needs of the target market **[1]**

8. A graphic designer has developed a new range of promotional brochures for a business company. Which combination is best suited for its success?

☐ A. Cost and durability

☐ B. Cost and aesthetics

☐ C. Aesthetics and function

☐ D. Durability and aesthetics **[1]**

9. At which point will a designer know if a product is viable?

☐ A. Manufacturing phase

☐ B. Market research on the current products

☐ C. Ideation phase

☐ D. Evaluation phase **[1]**

10. How can sustainable design be achieved?

☐ A. Making designs innovative for the consumers

☐ B. Making durable products

☐ C. Making competitive products in the marketplace

☐ D. Making products that are environmentally friendly by using a minimum amount of resources **[1]**

Remember to mark your chosen answer clearly. If you change your mind cross it out obviously and mark up your new answer.

The exams are not designed to trick you. Don't panic on the day. Remind yourself that you know how to answer the questions.

If you are getting stuck on a question, try moving on and coming back to it later.

Don't spend too much time on just one question. Don't over think it and confuse yourself. Leave it, flag it to yourself and come back to it.

Three answer choices include the use of 'aesthetics'. Think about your answer carefully.

Practise your critical and analytical skills as you review.

Review your study material frequently to maintain a good grasp of the content.

Do not confuse the concepts of eco-design, green design and sustainable design.

11. What is the objective of designing products for comfort?

☐ A. Creating a product mainly targeted at the older population groups

☐ B. Creating a product targeted at people with a disability

☐ C. Designing products that are complex to use

☐ D. Improving productivity or efficiency **[1]**

12. What is the role of an entrepreneur in adding value to a designer's work?

☐ A. Expanding economic activity by promoting new products

☐ B. Managing costs for the production of the new products

☐ C. Taking financial risks to promote innovative products

☐ D. Accepting responsibility for design refinement **[1]**

Application of product ergonomics improves the productivity.

13. Why does intellectual property need to be protected?

☐ A. It allows competing designers to collaborate effectively

☐ B. It ensures that ideas cannot be promoted or traded by other designers

☐ C. It supports designer's ideas to be known locally and internationally

☐ D. It guarantees that all future designs are effectively patented **[1]**

Remember it is important you are aware of current changes and developments in the design technology market.

14. A designer has created an automatic clothes-ironing machine. What should be their strategy to evaluate its ease of use?

☐ A. Receive feedback from subject-matter experts

☐ B. Investigate the selection of manufacturing supplies

☐ C. Conduct user and market research

☐ D. Trial it using different user groups **[1]**

Look for key words or phrases. Here 'ease of use' is important.

15. Which factors decide the usefulness of a design?

☐ A. The values and opinions of the users

☐ B. The level of expertise and resources available

☐ C. How much it meets the requirements of end-use

☐ D. The use of integrated elements and the principles of design **[1]**

Usability is about how easy it is to use a product for the users.

16. What is a chief feature of entrepreneurial activity?

☐ A. Conducting a suitable marketing campaign and life-cycle assessment

☐ B. Identifying opportunities and risk taking

☐ C. Designing the manufacturing system of a product

☐ D. Studying emerging technologies **[1]**

Do not spend more than a minute for questions you are very sure with. A tricky question should take you a maximum of two minutes. Try to save ten minutes for proofreading your answers at the end.

17. How does a designer investigate the target market of a product?

☐ A. Employ a financier to assess the product

☐ B. Make a prototype of the product for the market and ask for feedback

☐ C. Assemble a focus group to conduct a survey of the product

☐ D. Use social media to get responses on the product **[1]**

Make sure you know the difference between target market and target audience.

18. When developing a new app, which combination of factors is most suitable?

☐ A. Governmental and legal consequences

☐ B. Social influence and developing technologies

☐ C. Marketing strategies and timing

☐ D. Financial and historical impacts **[1]**

Calculators are not allowed but you might be expected to carry out simple calculations.

19. Why is it essential for a designer to communicate with the customer?

☐ A. To adjust design ideas

☐ B. To improve brand appreciation

☐ C. To develop consumer satisfaction

☐ D. To collect opinion to encourage sales **[1]**

Imagine you are the customer. What information would you exchange with the designer?

20. Which of the following factor pairs influence the success of any innovation in the marketplace?

☐ A. Public demand and social values

☐ B. Inexpensive manufacturing processes

☐ C. Product requirement and cultural implications

☐ D. Timing and effective marketing approaches **[1]**

Successful innovations typically start with detailed design and marketing specifications.

21. A designer decides to develop a new product in the market. Which of the following is the most ethically sound concern?

☐ A. Accepting the social aspects of the society

☐ B. Reducing the environmental impacts and increasing the sustainability concerns for the producer

☐ C. Improving the lifestyles and workplace practices of the stakeholders

☐ D. Increasing the sales of the product to make profit for the manufacturer **[1]**

Being ethically sound is behaving in a way that demonstrates moral principles which are consistent with societal norms.

22. What is a direct relationship between obsolescence and the development in products?

☐ A. It boosts the usage of novel technologies

☐ B. It creates competition in the existing markets within similar products

☐ C. It safeguards the creation of ecological products

☐ D. It confines the produce of a producer **[1]**

Obsolescence is when a product is outdated and no longer used as newer products have taken over the market.

23. What is an important consideration for a designer with respect to industrial and commercial practices used during the manufacturing of a product?

☐ A. To guarantee the product will make a good profit for the company

☐ B. To admit the use of cheaper resources

☐ C. To design products meeting consumer needs

☐ D. To increase the rate of production of the product **[1]**

Consider industrial and commercial practices. What differences does each make?

24. Why is user-centric design approach important?

☐ A. It helps to develop designing strategies

☐ B. It safeguards the copyrights of the designer

☐ C. It helps the designer to understand the customer needs

☐ D. It encourages the usage of new technologies **[1]**

Dematerialization and design for manufacturing approaches are aimed towards reducing the amount of energy and materials used in the production process which have a direct environmental effect.

25. What contributes to the sustainability of a product during its production?

☐ A. Considering the commercial aspects

☐ B. Using the design for the manufacturing approach to minimize the effect of materials and processes on the environment

☐ C. Examining the energy required in its production

☐ D. Studying the recyclability of the materials to minimise wastage **[1]**

For more information on user-centric design, search for articles by Tim Brown, CEO and the president of IDEO.

Datschefski's five principles of sustainable design are: cyclic, solar, safe, efficient and social.

26. A kitchen shear design was trialled in 300 homes. Which of the following strategy is best suited to collect the data findings on the shear?

☐ A. Personal interview at each home

☐ B. Collect reviews from e-commerce websites

☐ C. Send a questionnaire to each home

☐ D. Observations on the use of the shear at each home **[1]**

> In this question it doesn't matter if you don't know what a kitchen shear design is, just think about the answers logically and which seems the most feasible.

27. Which factor is most substantial in the accomplishment of a marketing plan?

☐ A. How much of the product there is

☐ B. Being thoughtful about the market segment

☐ C. Use of social media

☐ D. Effectual packaging of the product **[1]**

> Don't forget to watch how much time you have left.

28. Which of the following characteristics represents an entrepreneur?

☐ A. Being robust

☐ B. Being a risk-taker

☐ C. Being lawfully responsible

☐ D. Being ecologically active **[1]**

> An entrepreneur is a person willing to use their own funds for a new enterprise even though this might mean losing money.

29. The evaluation stage in the design cycle of a product implicates a test of its qualities and functions. Why is it crucial to conduct this evaluation?

☐ A. To decide the product's aesthetic value

☐ B. To confirm that the desired operations are performed by the product

☐ C. To guarantee maximum selling of the product

☐ D. To decide if the product is a worthy solution to the design problem stated by the user **[1]**

> Market sector analysis is very important for a product's initial and continual success as it influences innovation and product development.

30. What does a user's design brief to a designer generally summarise?

☐ A. A fundamental design feature

☐ B. A list of all the legal necessities and budget objectives

☐ C. A summary of all limitations to be studied in the design

☐ D. A list of main environmental concerns **[1]**

> A successful design brief is based on understanding the users' needs and limitations.

31. Why is there a need in the current generation to develop sustainable technologies?

☐ A. To decrease the e-waste generated in landfills

☐ B. To make effective use of natural resources

☐ C. To make durable products

☐ D. To promote dematerialisation **[1]**

> Remember the circular economy concept.

32. A designer is asked to design a product that is user friendly to a variety of diverse cultures. What should be the chief consideration?

☐ A. Aiming towards the needs of the societies

☐ B. Developing a product that is appropriate for all market sectors

☐ C. Categorizing separate marketplace segments

☐ D. Using native workers in the production **[1]**

> Sustainable technologies are based on sustainable development goals which are aimed towards satisfying the human needs for resources of the current and the future generations without compromising the capacity of the planet.

33. What does a life-cycle analysis of a product predict?

☐ A. Manufacturing difficulties during the production

☐ B. The effect of the product on humanity and the ecosystem

☐ C. The cost of overproduction and inappropriate processing

☐ D. Disposal and the recyclability of materials **[1]**

> Remember that 'life-cycle analysis' is the way to assess all the environmental impacts throughout a product's life.

34. What opportunities do emerging technologies provide consumers with?

☐ A. Products that are innovative

☐ B. Products that have existing features which are successful in the market

☐ C. Products that guarantee sustainable choices

☐ D. Products that have a reduced scope of inherent functions **[1]**

> Emerging technologies are new to the market and their potential is still yet to be realized.

35. How is a design solution reflected to be most suitable?

☐ A. When it fulfils the visual appeal

☐ B. When it delivers strength, endurance and safety

☐ C. When it meets the needs of the market

☐ D. When it achieves the end-user's desires **[1]**

> A user-driven solution is one which satisfies the needs of the end user.

36. A new laptop sleeve is being designed. To meet the functional requirements, what criteria should be considered?

☐ A. Colour, weight and size

☐ B. Cost, ease of use and being stylish

☐ C. Weight, size and ease of use

☐ D. Material, appeal and price **[1]**

> Be careful when the same key words have been used in multiple answer choices. Make sure you choose the correct one.

37. How does a design team evaluate a product's viability after its proposal and prior to production?

☐ A. Creating a prototype to test the functionality and aesthetics

☐ B. Estimating the overall price of the product

☐ C. Comprehensively researching the previous and existing markets

☐ D. Studying the materials needed to make the product **[1]**

> A practical function is mostly concerned with the criteria associated with the performance of the product. This could be dimensions, weight or ease of use.

38. What purpose do scale models provide?

☐ A. To depict the technique of construction

☐ B. To offer an effectual method of communicating the ideas to others

☐ C. To determine the visual aspects of the project

☐ D. To guarantee working sketches of the project **[1]**

> Physical models of products allow designers to improve product user interface.

39. What contributes to developing a high-quality product?

☐ A. Using suitable manufacturing practices

☐ B. Applying eco-friendly manufacturing processes

☐ C. Evaluating accessible government allowances

☐ D. Developing functional or aesthetic features **[1]**

> Previous questions you have answered may help you to work out other answers.

40. At the end of a product life cycle, which factor adds to its decline in acceptance?

☐ A. Bad design

☐ B. Better materials

☐ C. Changing social trends

☐ D. Varying manufacturing practices **[1]**

> You should now have some time left to go back to questions you missed out and do a quick review of your answers, checking you haven't made any small errors.

> If you really don't know the answer to a question then you might as well make a guess when you go through at the end of the exam.

Paper 2: Standard Level/Higher Level

Set your timer to 1 hour 30 minutes.

This paper is worth 50 marks.

Section A

Answer **all** the questions in Section A.

1. Toyota Motor Corporation is a Japanese automotive manufacturer that has been in business for over 85 years. Toyota has a vision of providing 'mobility for all' of humankind, giving users the freedom to move despite a lack of roads, legs or even sight. They have provided innovations in mobile solutions by introducing the Toyota i-Tril, Concept-i and the i-Road, which uses artificial intelligence to provide safety and comfort to its users in an eco-friendly way.

Figure 1: A Toyota concept vehicle

   (a) (i) Some innovations are more successful than others. Outline why this could be. **[2]**

In section A, there is a data-based question that requires you to examine the given set of data. The remaining part of section A is made up of several short-answer questions.

Read the information carefully and make sure you refer back to the correct figure in any answers you give.

OUTLINE
You are required to take an idea and develop it with a brief explanation.

Questions that ask you to outline an idea are testing AO2.

Compare/contrast what you agree/disagree with and why.

Try thinking of an innovation that you know. Why did it become popular or why did it fail?

ANSWER ANALYSIS
This question is worth 2 marks, so you don't need to write a long essay for your answer.

(ii) Identify the ethical considerations taken into account while designing the mobility solutions at Toyota. **[2]**

Questions in the exam that expect you to identify a principle are testing your understanding of AO1.

Stay focused on the question. A general answer about ethical considerations will not get you full marks.

(b) 'Design is an iterative process and designers have a role in the continual improvement of the previous designs, even when the product is already operational, easy to use and cost efficient.'
Justify the above statement. **[4]**

JUSTIFY
Use relevant information to support your idea.

Don't panic if you don't fill up all of the answer space. As long as your answer has enough detail for the amount of marks then you can be confident.

Practise with study groups which may help you in brainstorming key points/perspectives or predict questions.

(c) Discuss how the use of sustainable materials stimulates the development of innovative products. [3]

(d) Discuss the legal responsibilities that the designers at Toyota might have considered whilst developing the mobility solutions for the community. [3]

DISCUSS

Write about your opinions or conclusions clearly. They need to be supported by appropriate evidence.

Look at the figures. Can you refer to them and include them in your answer?

What sustainable products can you think of? Bring some of your own knowledge into your answer to make a fully rounded response.

Remember you can format your answer into detailed bullet points if it helps you to form your answers more coherently and accurately.

What legal responsibilities can you think of? If you were the designer what would you consider?

Limit your personal feelings unless specifically asked for.

Remember to look back at the text provided at the beginning of the case study to help you answer the short questions.

This tests AO3. You need to present a balanced view.

With 3-mark answers it is important to ensure you include three solid, separate points to create a strong answer.

(e) A designer has developed two chairs for different uses.

Figure 4: Office chair

Figure 5: Modern bar chair

(i) List the three human factors that a designer remembers while designing products to meet ergonomic needs. **[3]**

....

....

....

....

....

(ii) Compare and contrast how human factors have been applied differently in the development of the two types of chair (Figures 4 and 5). **[3]**

....

....

....

....

....

....

....

....

....

....

....

....

....

....

....

....

When answering a question worth fewer marks, do not go into detail. Include a specific point (or points) supported by specific details and examples.

Study the basic terminologies as they may appear frequently in the essay questions.

You may answer in single words for your answer when you are expected to list a particular thing.

Think about what each chair will be used for. For example, an office chair will need to get in and out from under desks easily.

ANSWER ANALYSIS

Use your answer from (i) to ensure you think about the three different human factors.

ANSWER ANALYSIS

You are being asked how the chairs are different, so you need to compare them. It is not enough to list their features.

2. (a) 'Form follows function' is a frequently used phrase. Outline why it is vital to consider a product's function in its development stage. **[2]**

....

....

....

....

....

....

(b) Discuss why designers often prefer conceptually sketching rather than computer-based designing. **[3]**

....

....

....

....

....

....

....

....

....

....

....

....

....

3. Describe how the advancements in technology have changed a design team's work practices. **[2]**

....

....

....

....

....

....

OUTLINE VS DISCUSS

'Outline' means you only need a brief summary on why it is important to consider a product's function in its development stage. 'Discuss' answers are balanced, include a range of arguments, and are supported by evidence.

While comparing and contrasting conceptual sketching over computer-based designing, make sure you learn the types of designing methods used in both with the advantages and disadvantages to discuss it appropriately.

In the guide there are a large number of command terms listed, but only a small number are used in the examination papers. Paper 2 uses lots of 3-marks clusters for AO3-type questions.

Make sure you have revised advancements in designing technology.

These might be positive or negative changes.

Make sure you describe the **impact** of advancements rather than just say what they are. You will need to focus on the impact that technological advancements have made on changing work practices for a design team (and not for the manufacturer, consumer, or anybody else).

4. Discuss the role of aesthetics in a consumer buying a product. **[3]**

Imagine you are the consumer. Do you buy a product based on how it looks visually or reviews you have read on how it works? Weigh up the different options and come to a critically analysed opinion to conclude.

When answering a question like this you may link the answer to the psychological response provoked by viewing the product.

The fundamental principle of 'form follows function' can be viewed from a customer's perspective.

Make sure you have revised aesthetic characteristics.

Make sure you include relationships between facts and concepts rather than just listing facts.

Highlight the key points in the question. Really think about what your answer should be focusing on. No marks will be given if you miss the point of the question.

Marks will be lost if your answer contradicts itself! Be careful of this while reviewing your answers.

Section B

Answer **only one** question from Section B.

5. Design teams often converge two or more technological systems to provide new functionality in a single product. For instance, a wearable smartphone frees users from handheld phones, wristwatches and wristband monitors.

Figure 6: Skin-based interface, wearable smartphone prototype

(a) Define converging technology. **[2]**

....

....

....

....

....

(b) List three different examples of products using converging technology. **[3]**

....

....

....

....

....

....

....

....

....

In this section, you need to select one question from a choice of three. The answers to the extended response questions may include writing a number of passages, solving a problem or carrying out an enquiry or evaluation.

Do not answer more than one section B question. Students who attempt all three section B questions generally perform poorly in that section of the paper.

When answering a question like this you may link the answer to the psychological response provoked by viewing the product.

Always remember to look for how many marks are being awarded for each question. This will give you a general idea of how much is expected from your answer.

The word converging is important here. Remember the example of a multifunctional printer (MFP) device. It performs several functions including printing, faxing, scanning and copying.

You could study the advantages and disadvantages of converging technologies.

The hints to some of the answers are also mentioned in the question. Make sure you carefully read the question and use the data given.

You will notice lots of AO3 questions in this paper. While answering these questions, remember:

- **One** correct main point plus three examples relating to it for 3 marks
- **Two** correct main points and three examples for each point for 6 marks
- **Three** main points and three examples for each point for 9 marks

(c) Discuss how products designed using converging technologies meet society demands. **[6]**

Questions in the exam that expect you to discuss a concept are testing your understanding of AO3.

Remember this section gives you a choice of three questions. Pick your question wisely. Select the one which you are most confident writing about.

Every topic appears almost easy when you are revising. However, you will realize whether you actually know the topic only after facing the sample papers.

You only answer one question in the exam but as part of your revision you should attempt to answer every question to continually build your knowledge. It will give you more confidence going into the exam.

Don't worry if you run out of space: you can ask for more paper during the exam.

If you are running out of time then don't be afraid to bullet point your answers so all your points are down on paper. Even if you haven't had a chance to analyse them properly you will still receive some marks.

Think about the environmental impact of any product during its life cycle. Does this demand responsibility from the engineers? What issues are currently prevalent and what are widening issues? Use your knowledge and ideas to create a rounded answer.

(d) With reference to social issues and Figure 6, analyse three impacts that products like this might have on society. **[9]**

ANALYSE

For answers which require you to carry out analysis, make sure you break down your facts into simple elements and structure.

ANSWER ANALYSIS

The question has asked for three impacts – remember the rule of three for a 9-mark question.

Read the question carefully. It is asking about issues, so you will not get any marks for analysing benefits.

HL students should have revised consumer attitudes and behaviours towards sustainability.

Another link to discuss social issues can be green legislation and implementing green design.

Analyse products designed using conventional technologies versus conventional technological products. Think about which is better, what you agree and disagree with, and why.

For a 9-mark question you will need to consider at least three societal issues and then explain the impact caused by each on the society to achieve maximum marks.

....

(lined answer space)

While answering essay questions include specific details and examples.

Make sure you include relationships between facts and concepts rather than just listing facts.

Remember the rule. Include either a concept, detail or example in your explanation for every mark the essay is worth.

6. 'Built-in obsolescence' or 'planned obsolescence' is a deliberate tactic used by designers to ensure the product has a limited 'lifespan' – meaning it is designed to be replaced rather than repaired. Refer to the following products which are designed for built-in obsolescence.

Figure 7: Outdated mobile phones

Figure 8: Typewriter

(a) List any two features of planned obsolescence. [2]

....

....

....

....

ANSWER ANALYSIS

The question asks for the two features – have you included two?

(b) Justify why designers develop products with planned obsolescence. **[3]**

JUSTIFY

Explain and rationalize the reasons and then give the reason which you think is the overall point as to why designers do this.

Justify the reason that designers adopt planned obsolescence, and talk about the advantages and disadvantages.

Make sure you know all the types of obsolescence.

You may consider an example of your own (such as MP3 players) while answering this question.

(c) Discuss the advantages and disadvantages associated with planned obsolescence. **[6]**

ANSWER ANALYSIS

The question asks for advantages and disadvantages, so make sure you include both.

Questions in the exam that expect you to discuss terminology are testing your understanding of AO3.

While studying the types of obsolescence think of one example of a product for each of the type. This may help you to recall it in the exam.

Think about why products have short life cycles. Is it due to the trends in new fashion? Latest technology? Or intentionally done to include new safety features?

(d) An understanding of a product's commercial life allows the designer to design a product with a shortened product cycle.

With reference to outdated mobile phones (Figure 7) and typewriters (Figure 8), discuss the impact that planned obsolescence might have on society, the environment, and the design process. **[9]**

Keep the answer clear. Avoid talking about each element of the question together as this presents an incoherent, muddled form of answer. Discuss each part of the question on its own.

Avoid writing an introduction as this just wastes time. You don't need a summary at the end either.

7. Green design integrates environmental considerations into the design of a product without compromising its integrity. Examples of green products made from eco-friendly materials are shown below:

Figure 9: Eco-friendly bag

Figure 10: Eco-friendly packaging

(a) Outline what green design refers to. [2]

....

....

....

....

(b) Explain the design objectives of green products. [3]

....

....

....

....

....

....

....

....

....

....

💬 **OUTLINE**
You are required to give a brief account of what green design refers to.

This tests your understanding of AO1. You only need to give a brief answer without an explanation. 🎯

! Beware of confusing similar terminologies you have studied. You may misread and confuse yourself between green design, eco design and sustainable design as all three have a common aim.

For a 3-mark question remember that using 'point-explanation-link' is a good approach to structuring an answer.

Understanding of concepts is more important than learning answer keys.

Review your analysing skills as you revise. For instance, why is it said that the timescale to implement green design is large?

(c) Describe how the use of eco-friendly materials and practices stimulate the development of innovative technologies. **[6]**

....

....

....

....

....

....

....

....

....

....

....

....

....

....

....

....

(d) Explain three opportunities and/or challenges faced by designers when attempting to design and produce green products. **[9]**

....

....

....

....

....

....

....

....

....

....

....

....

....

When answering an extended response question, always look at the marks awarded. Try to write as many points down as there are marks, more if possible in the time you have.

Students who prepare well for all the six core topics and Topic 4 specifically will be able to accomplish higher grades in both the sections of Paper 2.

As a manufacturer, how will you benefit from promoting the 'green' credentials that you have used in your latest innovations?

Imagine yourself to be a designer. What can be the possible challenge for you to design a green product? Will finding an alternative to existing designs or inventing a totally new design/material be challenging?

Do you think there is a pressure from the consumer end demanding for green products? If so, is it an opportunity or challenge for the manufacturers?

While responding to questions that use higher order command terms such as compare, discuss, explain and suggest you need to think beyond the boundaries of standard text book content and include material that goes beyond that provided in the context.

Revise all the design strategies and objectives for green products in order to know enough points for case studies regarding green design.

Be concise with your answers. Make good use of short structured statements in distinct paragraphs. Long sentences and large masses of text can become repetitive and tend to go off course.

EXPLAIN

Make a point and then develop it with reasoning.

Explain questions test AO3.

Paper 3: Higher Level

Set your timer to 1 hour 30 minutes.

This paper is worth 40 marks.

Section A

Answer **all** the questions given.

Use of calculators is allowed.

1. Plantbottle packaging is an innovation from The Coca-Cola Company, which is aimed at making the world look more positively on the waste produced from plastic bottles. Plantbottle is made through a process that turns sugarcane into a key component of PET plastic and is the first PET plastic beverage bottle made partially from plants that is completely recyclable. It functions like a normal PET plastic but has a smaller carbon footprint. Sustainable innovations like the Plantbottle have a major influence on the sustainable development of the planet.

Figure 1: Plantbottle™ make plastic bottles partially out of plants

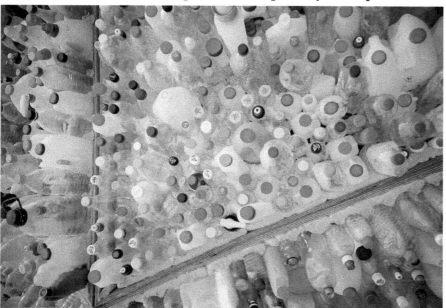

   (a) Describe the role of designers in sustainable development. [2]

....

....

....

....

....

....

....

....

Don't spend too much time on small-mark questions, you don't want to risk missing out on the high-mark questions throughout the paper.

Remember to make use of all the important information, diagrams, graphs and photographs in the examination paper.

Do not repeat the question in the answer.

(b) Describe sustainable innovation. [2]

....

....

....

....

....

....

....

(c) Outline what triple bottom line sustainability is. [2]

....

....

....

....

....

....

....

(d) Describe any four of Datschefski's five principles of sustainable design. [4]

....

....

....

....

....

....

....

....

....

....

....

....

....

....

2. Fitness bands are wearable wireless computing devices. They are worn on a person's wrist and are designed to track physical activity. As well as telling the time, the devices include activity trackers, which measure the user's data, such as the number of steps walked, stairs climbed, heart rate, quality of sleep, and other personal fitness metrics. It is part of a revolution in digital health.

Figure 2: Fitness bands

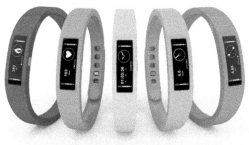

Figure 3: Displaying a user's physical activity

(a) Define user-centred design. **[2]**

....

....

....

....

(b) List any two strategies of user research essentially needed to be considered by the manufacturers of fitness bands. **[2]**

....

....

....

....

(c) Define inclusive design. **[2]**

....

....

....

....

(d) Describe four of the five stages of user-centred design. **[4]**

....

....

....

....

....

....

....

....

Do you use a fitness band? Consider your own experiences.

Questions in the exam that expect you to define a term are testing your understanding of AO1.

LIST
Give a number of possible answers. Each is worth 1 mark.

Who is the target audience of inclusive design?

ANSWER ANALYSIS
Check you have included four of the stages.

ANSWER ANALYSIS
Make sure you use appropriate IB DT terminology, vocabulary and definitions, and apply them to the framework of the explaining asked.

Section B: Case study on Ultraboost X Parley shoes

3. Corporate companies innovate ways to use business as a force for good. The fast-growing threat of marine plastic is polluting water and killing animals at a higher rate than ever before. In order to address this problem and build a more sustainable business plan, Adidas collaborated with a non-profit pioneering environmental organization: 'Parley for the ocean'. The outcome was the development of the eco-innovative material OCEAN PLASTIC®, which is used to make sneakers that have the equivalent of eleven plastic bottles in a single pair.

   The objective is to create a change by ceasing production of new plastic products and using upcycled marine plastic waste instead. The collaboration developed the Parley AIR strategy, arguing that everyone has a role to play in tackling the problem of ocean waste.

   AVOID plastic wherever possible

   INTERCEPT plastic waste

   REDESIGN the material itself

Figure 4: Marine plastic waste

Figure 5: Animals dying due to plastic pollution

Figure 6: Large brands have created sneakers from recycled ocean waste

(a) Outline a pioneering strategy. [2]

....

....

....

....

....

(b) Parley has developed the eco-innovative material called Ocean Plastic®
and registered the trademark. Outline why it is important for companies to
register their innovations. [2]

....

....

....

....

....

(c) Describe the market segmentation groups based on consumers' attitudes
towards green design. [2]

....

....

....

....

....

OUTLINE
Briefly give an account of a pioneering strategy.

This question tests AO2.

The launch of the iPad is an example of a pioneering strategy.

Do not memorize previous mark schemes. Focus on the key contexts and concepts the current question is asking for.

The answer is worth two marks so you need to include two points.

(d) Adidas' collaboration and partnership with Parley for the oceans contributes towards its corporate social responsibility programme. With reference to Figures 4–6, discuss why it is important for corporate companies to undertake such social activities. **[5]**

(e) Explain any three strategies used for setting the price of a product. **[9]**

EXPLAIN

Give a detailed account of the strategies. You are not being asked for your opinion.

In the 9-mark long-response question, you are encouraged to include three distinct points per aspect for a total of nine.

Set B

Paper 1: Standard Level

Set your timer to 45 minutes.

This paper is worth 30 marks.

Answer **all** the questions in this paper.
For each question, choose the answer you think fits the best.

A designer is developing the interior of a cockpit and wants to confirm that the pilot has easy access to all the controls.

Figure 1: The cockpit from inside an aeroplane

1. What type of data should the designer gather?
   - ☐ A. Secondary data
   - ☐ B. Dynamic data
   - ☐ C. Static data
   - ☐ D. Primary data [1]

2. What does it mean to reuse a product?
   - ☐ A. Implementation of the 'take back' idea
   - ☐ B. Action or practice of not using something again
   - ☐ C. The refurbishment of any portion of a product
   - ☐ D. Action or practice of using something to fulfil a different function (repurposing) [1]

Primary data collection involves users to conduct research by oneself for the purpose it is planned for. Secondary data collection allows users to collect research data which is conducted by a third party.

Reuse reduces the strain on valuable natural resources. It also creates a lower carbon footprint than manufacturing a new product.

3. Which statement is true about end-of-pipe technology?

☐ A. It reduces pollution

☐ B. It is an affluent treatment prior to discharge into the atmosphere

☐ C. It provides a substitute to non-renewable resources

☐ D. It improves the productivity of the process   **[1]**

Examples of some end-of-pipe technology solutions can be electrostatic precipitators, scrubbers and filters.

4. Look at Figure 2 below.

Figure 2: A technical drawing of a simple part

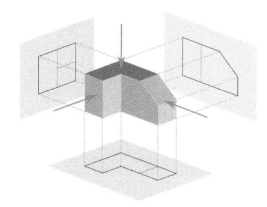

What is the style of the drawing in Figure 2?

☐ A. Isometric projection

☐ B. Orthographic projection

☐ C. Three-point perspective

☐ D. Assembly drawing view   **[1]**

Isometric projections are 3D drawings and orthographic projections are 2D drawings.

5. In the development of a mini cordless drill, a designer creates a model that gathers data relating to the drill configuration.

Figure 3: A mini cordless drill

What type of model has been created?

☐ A. A functional model

☐ B. An instrumented model

☐ C. A mock-up model

☐ D. A conceptual model   **[1]**

Instrumented models are developed to obtain accurate quantitative feedback for analysis.

6. What is an advantage of using man-made timber instead of natural timber?

☐ A. Large sheets of reliable quality can be easily manufactured

☐ B. High-tensile strength in all types of environments

☐ C. More recycle friendly

☐ D. Acts as the best renewable resource **[1]**

7. Which of the following are characteristics of polyethylene terephthalate (PET) fabric?

I High elasticity

II High absorbency

III High durability

☐ A. I and II only

☐ B. I and III only

☐ C. II and III only

☐ D. I, II and III **[1]**

> Make sure you read every choice carefully when you feel an MCQ is tricky.

8. What is the ethical and social impact of the increasing development of automation?

☐ A. Reduced labour costs

☐ B. Reduced production costs

☐ C. High leisure time

☐ D. Increased unemployment **[1]**

9. Which type of individual undertakes a financial risk in the hope of a profit during the development of a product?

☐ A. An innovator

☐ B. An entrepreneur

☐ C. A product champion

☐ D. A designer **[1]**

> A few examples of leading technology entrepreneurs are Jeffrey Bezos (CEO of Amazon) and Tim Cook (CEO of Apple).

10. The type of radio shown in Figure 4 was a popular kind of audio device. Such devices are rarely used today due to the creation of digital music players.

Figure 4: An old-style radio

> Reasons for obsolescence can be due to style, function and technology.

Which of the following is the reason for a lack of these radios in the marketplace?

☐ A. Style obsolescence

☐ B. Technological obsolescence

☐ C. Planned obsolescence

☐ D. Functional obsolescence **[1]**

11. User affordance is the way users perceive the usability of the product. Why is this important in usability testing?
 □ A. It shows why an object should be used
 □ B. It shows how an object should be used
 □ C. It shows when an object should be used
 □ D. It shows where an object should be used   [1]

> An example of 'user affordance': even if you have never seen a coffee mug before, its use is obvious.

12. 'Take back' is the idea that companies that make and sell the product are responsible for taking the product back after the consumers are done with it. Governments of many countries have now introduced this legislation to take back electronic products at the end of their life. Why are governments imposing such legislation?
 I   To decrease the waste going to landfill
 II To encourage retrieval of non-renewable resources
 III To generate a marketplace for second-hand electronics
 □ A. I, II and III
 □ B. I and II only
 □ C. I and III only
 □ D. II and III only   [1]

> Read the whole question carefully – don't skim it – before you attempt to answer. You don't want to miss any vital information.

13. What helps in evaluating a product's unsafe impact on the environment?
 □ A. Eco design
 □ B. Life-cycle analysis
 □ C. Sustainable design
 □ D. Green design   [1]

> In an industry regulated with take back legislation, the manufacturer is responsible for collection and treatment of all the products discarded by their customers, not the government.

14. Which would be the biggest challenge when designing a new (automobile) car?
 □ A. Ensuring it is aesthetically pleasing
 □ B. Ensuring it fulfils the related safety regulation
 □ C. Ensuring it is compatible with different fuel systems
 □ D. Ensuring it is suitable for a wide user group   [1]

15. Why does the design cycle often seem difficult to understand?
 □ A. Because it has a serial order
 □ B. Because it has complex stages
 □ C. Because it has an iterative nature
 □ D. Because it is a linear process   [1]

> Iterative design is the process of continual improvement of a concept, design or product.

16. Which of these methods for generating ideas requires collaboration in a team?
 □ A. Brainstorming
 □ B. Analogy
 □ C. Adaptation
 □ D. Attribute listing   [1]

17. Which model can be most suitable for demonstrating an original product to the general public?
 □ A. Scale model
 □ B. Graphical model
 □ C. Physical model
 □ D. Flowchart   [1]

18. Plastic building blocks are made from an injection moulding process.

Figure 5: Plastic blocks

Which factors are most important in the design of the plastic blocks?

I Design for disassembly

II Design for materials

III Design for process

☐ A. I and II

☐ B. I, II and III

☐ C. I and III

☐ D. II and III   **[1]**

19. Which term defines a mixture of two or more constituents with one acting as the glue?

☐ A. Composite

☐ B. Glulam

☐ C. Atom

☐ D. Alloy   **[1]**

20. Which material property would be needed in the tyre-pressure sensors of a car?

☐ A. Shape memory alloy

☐ B. Electro-rheostatic

☐ C. Magneto-rheostatic

☐ D. Piezoelectric   **[1]**

> Research the terms given as part of the answer options, so you get a better understanding of what the question is asking.

21. What is the percentile range that a stylist needs to consider during the production of mass-produced clothing?

☐ A. 5th

☐ B. 5th–95th

☐ C. 50th

☐ D. 95th   **[1]**

> Read the question clearly. You need to consider the mass production of clothing.

22. What is the benefit of using nuclear power?

☐ A. Fewer safety concerns

☐ B. Low contracting costs

☐ C. High energy density

☐ D. Waste product storage issues   **[1]**

> Read the confusing answers twice as they are only partly correct.

23. Which of the following describes identifying an unsatisfactory product or process to redesign and improve its performance?

☐ A. Brainstorming

☐ B. Constructive discontent

☐ C. Product research

☐ D. Attribute listing **[1]**

24. Which characteristic is true of both a lone inventor and a product champion?

☐ A. Strong corporate power

☐ B. Commitment to the product

☐ C. Creative by nature

☐ D. Business expertise **[1]**

A lone inventor and a product champion are not the same thing.

25. Which of the following is not a likely driver for green design?

☐ A. Health and safety aspects

☐ B. Benchmarks

☐ C. Customer pressure

☐ D. Cost-effectiveness **[1]**

26. Which of the following percentile ranges would be applicable in the mass production of an adjustable storage bench?

☐ A. 5th–95th

☐ B. 5th–50th

☐ C. 1st–99th

☐ D. 50th–95th **[1]**

27. A leading electronic company is rebuilding its electric motors for reselling. What is this an example of?

☐ A. Refurnishing

☐ B. Recycling

☐ C. Reconditioning

☐ D. Repairing **[1]**

If you are struggling to understand what the key terms mean then read the answer options and you might be able to figure it out.

28. Corporate houses use glass facades in their architecture. Which type of glass is best for this use?

Figure 6: Glass facades

☐ A. Soda-lime glass

☐ B. Laminated glass

☐ C. Tempered or toughened glass

☐ D. Pyrex or Borosilicate glass **[1]**

Research these terms and find an example where each type of glass is used. This will help deepen your understanding.

TEST: SET B PAPER 1 (SL)

51

29. Figure 7 shows a hardwood boat. Hardwood surfaces can be finished with a range of finishes such as shellac.

Figure 7: A hardwood boat

What is the drawback of applying shellac for finishing the surface of the boat?

☐ A. Reduces toughness

☐ B. Subject to scratching

☐ C. Glossy aesthetics

☐ D. Decreases moisture resistance   **[1]**

> Wood finishing is a process of applying a special kind of liquid to the surface of wood. This acts as a protective layer when it dries and enhances its protection and aesthetic appeal.

30. A manufacturing process of an automobile company has an end-of-pipe solution.

Figure 8: A manufacturing line

Which of the choices below is an incorrect statement about the solution?

☐ A. It is in agreement with green design principles

☐ B. The waste and emissions from the manufacturing process is recognised

☐ C. It is a progressive attitude to clean technology

☐ D. It increases the difficulty of an automobile manufacturing process   **[1]**

Paper 1: Higher Level

Set your timer to 1 hour.

This paper is worth 40 marks.

Answer **all** the questions in this paper.
For each question, choose the answer you think fits the best.

1. A smart watch is a wearable computer in the form of a wristwatch. It provides an interface between a smartphone and the wearable software.

    Figure 1: A smart watch

    What type of innovation is best to describe the smart watch system?
    ☐ A. Technological push
    ☐ B. Modular innovation
    ☐ C. Configurational innovation
    ☐ D. Architectural innovation   [1]

    Make sure you study the different types of innovation whilst finding examples. This will help deepen your understanding and select the right option in the exam.

2. 'A leadership figure determines larger goals that filter down to the tasks of lower-level employees to assist in developing ideas to meet these goals.' What business approach is this describing?
    ☐ A. Product stewardship
    ☐ B. Top down
    ☐ C. Bottom up
    ☐ D. Delayering   [1]

    Top-down strategies are strategies implemented from the 'top', such as global or national government initiatives.

3. Which of the following is most suitable for the manufacturing of a cricket bat and ball?

Figure 2: A cricket bat and ball

☐ A. Continuous flow production
☐ B. Batch production
☐ C. One-off production
☐ D. Mass production   **[1]**

4. What is the benefit of utilising computer numerical control (CNC) technology in an automatic production system?
☐ A. Condensed waste
☐ B. Increased investment
☐ C. Reduced expenditures
☐ D. Improved efficiency   **[1]**

5. Triple bottom line sustainability is a concept that broadens a business focus by including social, economical and environmental considerations. Which is the most important consideration for a manufacturer?
☐ A. Legal
☐ B. Environmental
☐ C. Economic
☐ D. Social   **[1]**

6. A product is being redesigned. Which evaluation strategy should a designer use to give them a detailed problem checklist on a product's usability?
☐ A. Focus groups
☐ B. User trial
☐ C. Survey methodology
☐ D. Usability testing   **[1]**

7. What statement is correct when talking about an eco-label and an energy label?
☐ A. It helps better decision-making in consumers
☐ B. It indicates that a product is designed with a high environmental standard
☐ C. It indicates that a product follows the principles of eco-design
☐ D. It is a compulsory international standard   **[1]**

To identify the correct production type, think about the demand the product has in the community.

For each of the processes think of examples of different products that get manufactured in each one.

While revising for any environmental consideration, study from the designer, manufacturer and consumers' perspective.

8. Which of the following approaches means continuous improvement?

☐ A. Lean production

☐ B. Kaizen

☐ C. Quality assurance

☐ D. Just-in-time manufacturing **[1]**

Understand the difference between an approach and a method/process.

9. Which steps of the user-centred design approach would involve potential users?

I Concept generation

II Execution

III Investigation

☐ A. I and II only

☐ B. I, II and III

☐ C. I and III only

☐ D. II and III only **[1]**

10. What is involved in a user-centred design approach?

I Advertising

II Observation

III Questionnaires

☐ A. I and II only

☐ B. II and III only

☐ C. I and III only

☐ D. I, II and III **[1]**

A user-centred design approach is a process led by users and developed through user-centred evaluation. Make sure you identify the objective of user involvement at each stage.

11. A manufacturer wants to decide the cost of their product. Which of the following defines the smallest price for a cost-effective product?

☐ A. Need for the product in the society

☐ B. Manufacturing costs

☐ C. Competition in the market

☐ D. Deduced value **[1]**

Think about what it means to be a manufacturer.

12. A working prototype is mandate for which of the following evaluation tests?

I User test

II Field test

III Performance test

☐ A. I, II and III

☐ B. I and III

☐ C. I and II

☐ D. II and III **[1]**

13. What is the benefit of shifting from just-in-case (JIC) to just-in-time (JIT) production?

☐ A. Less transporting of goods

☐ B. Prevents overproduction of materials

☐ C. Shorter waiting periods

☐ D. Less defects in production **[1]**

Read the question carefully. It is asking for the benefit of JIT production, not of JIC production.

14. For a manufacturer, the maximum flexibility is found in which of the scales of production?

☐ A. Craft

☐ B. Mass production

☐ C. Mechanization

☐ D. Automation **[1]**

15. Consumer attitude is highly important within the context of marketing. Which group of consumers strongly support environmentally friendly practices?

☐ A. Eco-warriors

☐ B. Eco-fans

☐ C. Eco-champions

☐ D. Eco-phobes **[1]**

16. The iPad is a product by Apple which combines productivity with affordability. Apple have released a new version of the iPad in order to improve sales in an existing market. Which corporate strategy is the company setting an example of?

☐ A. Product development

☐ B. Product diversification

☐ C. Market penetration

☐ D. Market development **[1]**

> A corporate strategy is a strategic plan of the company which defines its future goals.

> Look for keywords. Here the words 'new version' are important.

17. What is a drawback of JIC production?

☐ A. Must hold the inventory for the manufacturing system

☐ B. A larger network of supply chain is needed

☐ C. The convenience of having buffer goods

☐ D. Able to regulate the demand and supply of the market **[1]**

18. What is the benefit of using Computer Integrated Manufacturing (CIM) in electronic design automation?

☐ A. Recovery of part designs is controlled by the system

☐ B. Production is traced by a computer which controls the inventory

☐ C. Prototypes are made by testing specifications in a virtual environment

☐ D. Components are ordered and traced by the computer system **[1]**

19. Which of the following is the stimulus for a planned obsolete product?

☐ A. Market pull

☐ B. Retro styling

☐ C. Technology push

☐ D. Product re-engineering **[1]**

20. Suggest a suitable plastic for the production of the electrical plug shown in Figure 3.

Figure 3: An electric plug

☐ A. Polyurethane

☐ B. Urea-formaldehyde

☐ C. Polyethylene terephthalate

☐ D. Polyvinyl chloride **[1]**

> Do you know what all the terms in the answer options mean? If not, research them – it will help you decide on your answer.

21. Which strategy of evaluation can a designer carry out in a laboratory?

☐ A. Field test

☐ B. Subject matter expert appraisal

☐ C. Performance test

☐ D. Interviews [1]

22. A chocolate retail store sells its products at $10.99, $18.99, $20.99 and $14.99 (USD). Which of the following pricing strategy has the retailer used?

☐ A. Cost-plus pricing

☐ B. Psychological pricing

☐ C. Competitor pricing

☐ D. Demand pricing [1]

> Any price ending with .99, .98 or even .49 is based on strategy of making a consumer psychologically pay less.

23. Engineered wood or composite wood is manufactured by binding or fixing veneers of wood together with adhesives. Which of the following composite wood is manufactured by gluing layers of veneers together?

☐ A. Chipboard

☐ B. Plywood

☐ C. MDF

☐ D. Particle board [1]

24. An environmental impact assessment matrix is used to identify the potential impact of a project on the environment. How is this useful for life-cycle analysis?

☐ A. It recognizes the duties of the designer

☐ B. It recognizes the most important environmental impacts

☐ C. It categorizes the materials for remaking

☐ D. It identifies design conflicts for resolution [1]

25. Which of the following is not a trait of a lone inventor?

☐ A. Business-like

☐ B. Inflexible

☐ C. Innovative

☐ D. Single-minded [1]

26. Polyvinyl Chloride (PVC) has some major applications in medical equipment. What would be a main disadvantage of using PVC for making such equipment?

> Use correct logic and reasoning to apply your understanding to different design situations.

Figure 4: Sterile blood collection tube

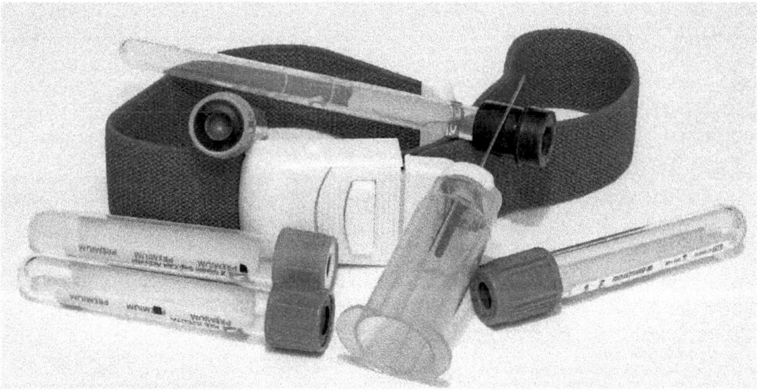

☐ A. Very costly

☐ B. Less moisture protection

☐ C. Hard to fabricate

☐ D. Difficult to recycle in comparison to other types of plastic [1]

27. During the study of the life-cycle analysis of an aircraft, which environmental concern is most significant?

☐ A. Soil pollution

☐ B. Air contamination

☐ C. Water

☐ D. Noise **[1]**

28. Which of the following materials is appropriate for manufacturing a seatbelt?

Figure 5: Seatbelt

☐ A. Silk

☐ B. Nylon

☐ C. Cotton

☐ D. Wool **[1]**

Research the latest material applications of every material. This will broaden your understanding.

29. In the design of the skin-cleansing brush shown in Figure 6, which of the physiological aspects are the inventors emphasizing?

Figure 6: A skin-cleansing brush

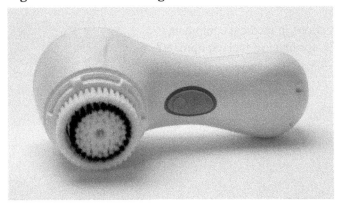

☐ A. Durability

☐ B. Comfort and Fatigue

☐ C. Biomechanics

☐ D. Affordance **[1]**

It is very essential to understand people's tolerances (physiological aspect) and design products which improves comfort and reduces fatigue while using them.

30. Which of the following is a conventional energy source?

☐ A. Solar energy

☐ B. Biomass

☐ C. Natural gas

☐ D. Hydro energy [1]

31. Timber is a non-self-renewable resource. When can it be defined as a renewable source?

☐ A. After it has been reused

☐ B. After it has been recycled

☐ C. After a tree is planted to replace the utilised timber

☐ D. After it is re-engineered [1]

32. A designer is commissioning a new green design project. What should be the aim of the project?

☐ A. People, planet, profit

☐ B. Materials, energy, pollution

☐ C. Reuse, recondition, repair

☐ D. Manufacturing, delivery, use [1]

33. Select the main benefit of reconditioning a bike.

☐ A. It makes the bike more energy efficient

☐ B. It lengthens the bike's life

☐ C. It is as dependable as a new bike

☐ D. It is safe to use [1]

34. Which statement is true regarding composites and alloys?

☐ A. Material groups can be joined

☐ B. The atomic number is the same

☐ C. Materials are joined to improve a particular material's property

☐ D. There is a fixed ratio of parent materials in joining [1]

35. Which of the following cannot be moulded by casting?

☐ A. Polymers

☐ B. Metal

☐ C. Timber

☐ D. Composites [1]

36. What is a 'goal' in a design challenge?

☐ A. The user of the product

☐ B. The final result

☐ C. The functional prototype

☐ D. The design specifications of the product [1]

37. Which of the following choices refer to materials, manufacturing and disassembly?

☐ A. Craft production

☐ B. Computer aided manufacturing (CAD)

☐ C. Design for manufacture (DfM)

☐ D. Batch production [1]

Do not confuse the concept of conventional and non-conventional energy.

Remember the circular economy concept.

Reconditioning is about rebuilding. A product may become 'new' in condition by repairing or replacing it with new parts.

Remember casting is a process which requires the raw material for manufacturing in a molten state.

38. What is the main characteristic of a cradle-to-cradle approach?

☐ A. Reconditioning

☐ B. Reusing

☐ C. Reducing

☐ D. Repairing **[1]**

39. What is the main objective of a conceptual sketch?

☐ A. To offer evidence of a new concept

☐ B. To communicate new ideas that are unfamiliar between the stakeholders

☐ C. To exhibit the drafting abilities of the designer

☐ D. To demonstrate a detailed working of a new idea **[1]**

40. Which expression defines a product well accepted in the market?

☐ A. Robust design

☐ B. Invention

☐ C. Innovation

☐ D. Dominant design **[1]**

A conceptual sketch allows you to visualise and express ideas easily.

A dominant design is one which has features that competitors and innovators have recognized as significant in the market.

Paper 2: Standard Level/Higher Level

Set your timer to 1 hour 30 minutes.

This paper is worth 50 marks.

Section A

Answer **all** questions. Answers must be written within the answer boxes provided.

1. The Vespa GTS (Granturismo Sport) 300 series is a range of scooter currently manufactured by Piaggio under the Vespa brand. It has a single cylinder four-stroke 300 HPE (high-performance engine) with an electronic-injection and liquid-cooling system. It has improved performance and reduced fuel consumption. To ensure it is safe to drive, it also has 12-inch tyres along with double-disk braking and ABS braking systems. This scooter is marked as a premium product and the manufacturer's suggested retail price (MSRP) is $7,099 (USD).

Figure 1 and 2: Different variations of scooters

Vespa is an expensive scooter brand due to the money spent in its research and development.

(a) (i) State the percentile range used to design the seat of the Vespa GTS 300.

[1]

(ii) Outline one ergonomic consideration about the design of the handlebars.

[2]

Imagine yourself using the handlebars. What considerations come to mind?

(b) (i) Figure 3 shows glass bottle packaging. State two characteristics which make glass a good packaging source. [2]

Figure 3: Glass bottle packaging

....

....

....

....

> These are only small-mark questions – don't spend too long writing detailed answers.

(ii) Outline the reason why plastic has largely replaced glass in the packaging industry. [2]

....

....

....

....

> Recent environmental movements are encouraging people to use less plastic. What do you think will replace plastic?

(c) (i) Outline what happens in the pre-production stage of life-cycle analysis. [2]

....

....

....

....

....

(ii) Explain the need of using the environmental assessment matrix from the perspective of a product designer. [3]

....

....

....

....

....

....

....

....

> Remember that an environmental assessment matrix is a list of environmental aspects against which we determine whether an activity would have an adverse effect, no effect or a beneficial effect.

(d) (i) List one type of plastic weld. **[1]**

....

....

(ii) Outline how permanent joining methods lead to planned obsolescence of the product. **[2]**

....

....

....

....

(e) (i) List two renewable energy sources. **[2]**

....

....

....

....

> Renewable energy sources are also called alternative energy sources.

(ii) Discuss one disadvantage of using a renewable energy resource as an alternative to fossil fuels. **[3]**

....

....

....

....

....

....

....

....

....

2. The Fender Stratocaster is a series of electric guitar designed in 1954 by Leo Fender, Bill Carson, George Fullerton and Freddie Tavares. The Fender Musical Instruments Corporation has continuously manufactured the Stratocaster from 1954 to the present. The casing is made of ash wood and alder wood mainly because of its lightweight and easy-to-finish properties. The Stratocaster has achieved iconic status and international recognition in the guitar industry.

Figure 4 and 5: Examples of electric guitars

(a) (i) List two features that make the Stratocaster a classic design. **[2]**

....

....

....

....

(ii) Describe how form follows function in the case of the Stratocaster series. **[2]**

....

....

....

....

You may answer in single words when you are only expected to list a particular thing.

3. **Figure 6** shows a driving car for toddlers which is made of aluminium material. The car has a mini steering system, a soft cushioned seat and a sound button for honking. The design team would have used a wide fidelity range of prototypes in the development of the car. It is likely that the design team would have used a physical model to easily identify any design problems and potential solutions within the context of space and the user needs of this product.

Figure 6: A car designed for toddlers

Explain why the design team would have chosen to use a physical modelling technique to test the ergonomic features of the car. **[3]**

....

....

....

....

....

....

....

4. Explain an advantage of a cradle-to-cradle philosophy over cradle-to-grave philosophy. **[3]**

....

....

....

....

....

....

Section B

Answer **one** question. Write in the space provided.

5. Many high-tech companies have switched to 3D printing to manufacture components for applications that are subject to a varied environment. MakieLab was one such company that let you design your own doll. The company 3D printed 10-inch flexile fashion dolls from thermoplastic. Customers got to choose all the features of the doll, such as the face, eyes, jaw or hair.

    The company started with a manufacturing plant in London, and shipped around the world. They marketed the product as environmentally friendly, not only because of the 3D printing process, which produced less waste, but because the packaging was made from recyclable materials.

Figure 7: Plastic dolls with different features

(a) Outline two benefits of using 3D printing in the manufacturing of a MakieLab fashion doll. **[2]**

....

....

....

....

....

....

....

Questions in the exam that expect you to outline a concept are testing your understanding of AO2.

(b) Outline why thermoplastics are used to produce a fashion doll. **[3]**

....

....

....

....

....

....

....

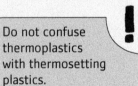

Do not confuse thermoplastics with thermosetting plastics.

(c) Explain how using plastic injection molding can reduce cost and waste during the production of fashion dolls. **[6]**

(d) Explain three drivers for green design that would lead MakieLab to develop environmentally friendly toys. **[9]**

....

....

....

....

....

....

....

....

....

....

....

....

....

....

....

....

....

6. Volvo is a Swedish multinational manufacturing company headquartered in Gothenburg. Its core activity is based in the production, distribution and sales of trucks, buses and construction equipment. It also develops autonomous driving technology and has tested many of its self-driving cars around the world. One example is the Volvo 7900, a fully autonomous and electric/hybrid bus being tested in Singapore for use as public transport.

The Volvo 7900 is a single decker accommodating 80 passengers and requires 80% less energy than a diesel-powered bus of equal size. It is controlled by AI navigation software along with an advanced global navigation satellite system.

Figure 9: Volvo 7900

(a) Outline why the innovation of the electric self-driving bus may be seen as an example of market pull. **[2]**

....

....

....

....

....

....

The term 'market pull' refers to the need for a new product or a solution to a problem which arises from the market place. The need is often identified by potential customers.

(b) Identify the human factors applied in designing the interior of the Volvo 7900. **[3]**

....

....

....

....

....

....

Imagine yourself designing the interiors of the vehicles. What considerations come to mind? Is it the seating? The ambiance? The comfort?

(c) Describe three design criteria for the Volvo 7900. **[6]**

....

....

....

....

....

....

....

....

....

....

....

....

....

....

....

....

....

....

....

Questions in the exam that expect you to describe a concept are testing your understanding of AO2.

(d) Explain the product life cycle of the electric/hybrid bus relative to its growth, planned obsolescence and its potential for further development as an innovation. **[9]**

If you are running out of time, don't be afraid to bullet-point your answers so all your points are down on paper. Even if you haven't had a chance to analyse them properly you will still receive marks.

Don't worry if you run out of space – you can ask for more paper during the exam.

7. **Figure 10** shows Vedel adjustable furniture for children. Kristian Solmer Vedel was a Danish industrial designer who developed this furniture set in 1951. This children's chair is made up of semi-circular bent plywood with slits to adjust the laminated plywood pieces. These pieces are held under tension without the use of any fitting, such as screws, nails or bolts. It can be adjusted into various arrangements, such as a chair, table or high chair. This means the design is easily adaptable and was intended to be useful throughout a child's upbringing.

Figure 10: Vedel's children furniture

Figure 11: Different angles of Vedel's furniture

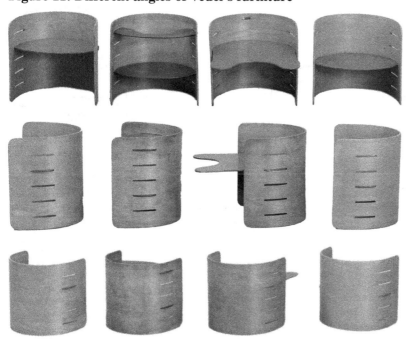

(a) Identify two techniques by which the concept of design for disassembly affects the success of Vedel's furniture set. **[2]**

....

....

....

....

....

(b) Analyse how the concept of tension in the chair design is relevant to the development of the wooden slits for adjustability. **[3]**

....

....

....

....

....

....

....

....

....

....

....

(c) Discuss how the designer applied anthropometric and physiological factors in the development of the chair. **[6]**

....

....

....

....

....

....

....

....

....

....

....

....

....

....

....

....

....

> Consider the two factors given in the question. Do they link? If not, why not? Look at the similarities and differences and how each factor works.

ANSWER ANALYSIS

This question has asked you about anthropometric and physiological factors. Make sure you talk about both of them.

d) Explain three features of plywood which play an important role in the
design of the chair. [9]

....

....

....

....

....

....

....

....

....

....

....

....

....

....

....

....

....

....

....

....

....

....

....

....

....

....

....

....

ANALYSE

For answers which
require you to carry
out analysis, make
sure you break down
your facts into simple
elements and structure.

Make sure
you study
the advantages and
disadvantages of plywood
to justify its role.

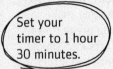

Paper 3: Higher Level

Set your timer to 1 hour 30 minutes.

This paper is worth 40 marks.

Section A

Answer **all** the questions given.

Use of calculators is allowed.

1. A skyTran is a public transport system concept first proposed by inventor Douglas Malewicki in 1990. The skyTran concept shown in Figure 1 uses ultra-light computer-controlled cars below aluminum maglev (magnetically levitated) tracks which can be supported above roads by use of poles.

   The skyTran combines the concepts of maglev and a hanging/minimalistic design, similar to the idea of Personal Rapid Transit (PRT) cars carrying individual passengers to their destinations. Being suspended in the sky would be a major benefit of skyTran, as taking users off the road would reduce traffic for people driving cars. Commercial implementation of this project would take place if testing proves to be successful.

   Figure 1: The pods would travel through the air rather than blocking the road

   (a) List two reasons why Personal Rapid Transits like skyTran can make the public transport system more efficient. **[2]**

   ....

   ....

   ....

   ....

   (b) Outline the need for a multidisciplinary design team for skyTran. **[2]**

   ....

   ....

   ....

   ....

Personal Rapid Transit (PRT) – also referred to as 'pod cars' – are vehicles designed for individual or small group travel carrying no more than three to six passengers.

ANSWER ANALYSIS

The question has asked you about the multidisciplinary design team for the skyTran. Make sure you stay focused on it.

(c) Outline the role of a psychologist in the design of the skyTran. **[2]**

....

....

....

....

....

....

> A psychologist is someone who studies the mind and emotions of a person and how they relate to behaviour.

(d) Describe how user experience in the skyTran could contribute towards its success. **[4]**

....

....

....

....

....

....

....

....

....

....

....

> A designer's ability to provide satisfaction through aesthetic appeal and pleasure can greatly influence the success of a product.

2. Sophie La Girafe is a toy for babies that is in the shape of a giraffe. It stimulates their five senses and is suitable from the age of three months. It is made from 100% natural rubber derived from the Hevea tree using the rotational moulding process. It is BPA free and painted with food-grade paint which makes it completely safe for teething babies to chew on, helping them relieve the pressure on their gums.

Sophie La Girafe is based on eco-design objectives and complies with the highest safety level for consumers. First manufactured in 1961, it has a sale of over 50 million units and is a huge success in the toy industry.

Figure 2: A Sophie La Girafe toy

(a) List two ways in which the toy can be considered an example of eco-design. **[2]**

....

....

....

....

....

....

(b) Discuss how the toy can be seen through the lens of ethical consumerism. **[3]**

....

....

....

....

....

....

....

(c) Define eco-design. **[2]**

....

....

....

....

....

(d) Explain how Sophie La Girafe balances material, health and usability consideration. **[3]**

ANSWER ANALYSIS

The question asks for the balance between material, health and usability. Make sure you talk about all three in the answer.

....

....

....

....

....

....

....

....

....

....

Section B

All questions are compulsory

3. People with respiratory or cardiovascular problems can use pulse oximeters, such as those shown in Figures 3 and 4. The oximeter is a clip-on device which measures the percentage of oxygen in the user's haemoglobin. This is called oxygen saturation and signifies how much oxygen is being supplied to the user's organs. All systems and organs in the body require oxygen; without it cells will begin to breakdown and ultimately die. Cell death can cause severe symptoms and eventually lead to organ failure.

The oximeter can be attached to a finger, wrist, foot or any other area where the device can read the person's blood flow around the body. It has been designed with the user in mind (user-centred design).

Figure 3 and 4: Pulse oximeters

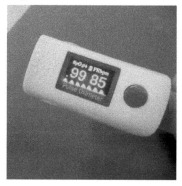 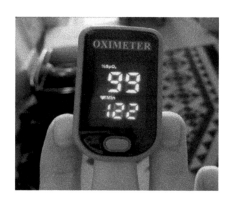

(a) List three marketing strategies that could have been used in the development of the oximeters. **[3]**

> Questions in the exam that expect you to list terminology are testing your understanding of AO1.

(b) Identify two roles of the users in this type of design approach. **[2]**

> While enlisting the role of users in the design approach, remember the five stages of UCD: research, concept, design, implementation and launch.

(c) The UCD approach requires designers to have a deep understanding of the user, task and environment in order to design successful products. Outline how the designers have applied **one** of these requirements (user, task and environment) to the oximeter. **[2]**

(d) Describe how learnability and attitude play an important role in the user-centered design objectives with respect to an oximeter. [4]

....

....

....

....

....

....

....

....

....

....

....

....

....

....

....

....

(e) Explain how the oximeter uses socio-pleasure, physio-pleasure and ideo-pleasure to satisfy its user. [9]

....

....

....

....

....

....

....

....

....

....

....

....

....

While answering an extended response question, always look at the marks awarded and the points asked. You may write unnecessary points and waste time. Or you may not write enough points to get full marks.

Set C

Paper 1: Standard Level

Set your timer to 45 minutes.

This paper is worth 30 marks.

Answer **all** the questions in this paper.
For each question, choose the answer you think fits the best.

NOTES

1. What is anthropometry?
   - ☐ A. The geometrical concerns of an object
   - ☐ B. The study of human behaviours
   - ☐ C. The dimensions of an object
   - ☐ D. The study of human body properties **[1]**

2. What is reconditioning?
   - ☐ A. A step when working on motors
   - ☐ B. The steps to keep a product functioning
   - ☐ C. The process by which products may be returned to their original manufactured specification
   - ☐ D. Making an initial design stronger **[1]**

3. What is a conceptual model?
   - ☐ A. A representation of what the user is likely to think and how the user is likely to respond
   - ☐ B. A representation that shows all finalized details
   - ☐ C. A CAD representative
   - ☐ D. A real representation **[1]**

4. What are the physical properties of a material?
   - ☐ A. Its strength
   - ☐ B. How it interacts with energy and matter
   - ☐ C. Its 3D aspects
   - ☐ D. What it looks like **[1]**

5. Patents, trademarks and copyright are examples of what?
   - ☐ A. Branding
   - ☐ B. Protection
   - ☐ C. Intellectual property
   - ☐ D. Marketing **[1]**

6. Which below is the best definition of retro design?
   - ☐ A. Designs that have historical relevance
   - ☐ B. Looking backwards at the design process
   - ☐ C. The means of looking at the design process retrospectively
   - ☐ D. Designs that evoke nostalgia revivals **[1]**

7. What is semiotics?

☐ A. Types of electronic symbols

☐ B. The study of signs and symbols

☐ C. The means of design communication

☐ D. A type of electronic device **[1]**

8. What are shelved technologies?

☐ A. A structural approach to design

☐ B. Essential technologies of importance

☐ C. Technologies that work with flatpack design

☐ D. When patent inventions are not commercially viable **[1]**

9. What is a smart material?

☐ A. A material that does not respond to external stimuli

☐ B. A material with one or more properties that can be dramatically altered

☐ C. A material that is used in space

☐ D. Material that has been considered carefully before choosing **[1]**

10. What is a piezoelectric material?

☐ A. Steel

☐ B. Copper

☐ C. A material that is sensitive to light

☐ D. A material that responds to the application of an applied stress **[1]**

11. Which option is the act of creating something new or of significant improvement?

☐ A. Invention

☐ B. Pioneer

☐ C. Trend

☐ D. Originality **[1]**

12. Which option describes creating radical solutions to problems in competitions with existing products?

☐ A. Innovative design

☐ B. Originality

☐ C. Disruptive innovation

☐ D. Breakthrough design **[1]**

13. What is virtual prototyping?

☐ A. A process that does not make use of simulation techniques

☐ B. The use of virtual reality (VR)

☐ C. 3D immersion

☐ D. A software-driven modelling process **[1]**

14. What does bottom-up modelling involve?

☐ A. Creating parts before joining them

☐ B. Capturing a new market sector

☐ C. A decline in demand and sales

☐ D. A product gaining acceptance and selling well **[1]**

NOTES

15. What is biomimicry?

☐ A. Using biotechnology

☐ B. Transferring a design from nature into design

☐ C. A design which mimics another

☐ D. A biological approach to design **[1]**

16. What is a technology push?

☐ A. When consumers drive change

☐ B. Technology that involves market research

☐ C. When technology adapts to market

☐ D. When innovative technological breakthroughs occur **[1]**

17. What is design for discomfort?

☐ A. Creating a situation that feels uncomfortable or has reduced comfort for limited time

☐ B. Creating a poor design

☐ C. An ergonomic principle

☐ D. Functional and aesthetically appealing design **[1]**

18. What is dematerialization?

☐ A. The selection of material

☐ B. A decline in material quality

☐ C. A reduction in production methods

☐ D. The progressive redirection in the amount of energy and/or material used in the production of a product **[1]**

19. What does circular economy refer to?

☐ A. The concept that: 'What is used, comes around'

☐ B. An economy based upon the use of renewable sources of energy

☐ C. Recycling

☐ D. The global use of a product **[1]**

20. What are percentile ranges?

☐ A. Nominal

☐ B. Ordinal

☐ C. Dividing a sample into 100 equal groups according to a particular variable

☐ D. Multiplying a product cost by the number of users **[1]**

21. What does physiological data refer to?

☐ A. Information gathering focusing on the funding of an individual major organ system

☐ B. Information referring to how people think in certain situations

☐ C. Information based on personal responses to stimuli

☐ D. Information tracking people's moods and attitudes **[1]**

22. What does embodies energy represent?

☐ A. An assessment of all energy misspent manufacturing a product

☐ B. An assessment of all energy not utilized in a product's use

☐ C. An assessment of all energy associated with a product throughout its life

☐ D. All energy tracked and recorded in the product process **[1]**

NOTES

23. What does cogeneration refer to?

☐ A. Generating two forms of energy from one source (electricity and heat)

☐ B. A theory about design thinking

☐ C. The operation of two generating sources working in parallel

☐ D. A measurement of rate of thinking **[1]**

24. What are end-of-pipe technologies?

☐ A. Metal-joining techniques

☐ B. A conventional approach to pollution reduction and waste

☐ C. Pipe-joining techniques

☐ D. Joining two different materials **[1]**

25. What is pultrusion?

☐ A. Another term for extrusion

☐ B. When material is repeatedly heated and cooled

☐ C. When material to be formed is pulled through a shaped dye

☐ D. When material is slowly cooled **[1]**

26. What are digital humans?

☐ A. Real-life users of virtual reality

☐ B. 2-dimensional mannequins

☐ C. Computer-based models used to assist researches in stimulating human biomechanics

☐ D. Robotic users **[1]**

27. What is Finite Element Analysis (FEA)?

☐ A. Testing virtual models under a variety of load conditions

☐ B. Analysing designs to finite degree

☐ C. Specifying quality assurance of models

☐ D. Testing designs to ascertain specific stresses **[1]**

28. What is shape memory?

☐ A. The term used to describe how a material changes once exposed to different temperatures

☐ B. A type of plastic, which once heated cannot be reformed

☐ C. Metals that exhibit pseudo-elasticity due to the rearrangement of their atomic lattice

☐ D. Materials that can regain their status once deformed **[1]**

29. What is psychological function?

☐ A. Wants that are driven by fads, fashion and technological needs

☐ B. An emotional attachment to a design

☐ C. A design that features purely in the mind

☐ D. Product testing to seek users' emotional responses **[1]**

30. What does a triadic colour scheme involve?

☐ A. Using one or two complementary colours

☐ B. Using a three-colour combination

☐ C. Using colours influenced by light

☐ D. Using a mixture of tertiary colours **[1]**

NOTES

Paper 1: Higher Level

Answer **all** the questions in this paper.
For each question, choose the answer
you think fits the best.

Set your timer to 1 hour.

This paper is worth 40 marks.

NOTES

1. What is anthropometry?
   - ☐ A. The geometrical concerns of an object
   - ☐ B. The study of human behaviours
   - ☐ C. The dimensions of an object
   - ☐ D. The study of human body properties **[1]**

2. What is reconditioning?
   - ☐ A. A step when working on motors
   - ☐ B. The steps to keep a product functioning
   - ☐ C. The process by which products may be returned to their original manufactured specification
   - ☐ D. Making an initial design stronger **[1]**

3. What is a conceptual model?
   - ☐ A. A representation of what the user is likely to think and how the user is likely to respond
   - ☐ B. A representation that shows all finalized details
   - ☐ C. A CAD representative
   - ☐ D. A real representation **[1]**

4. What are the physical properties of a material?
   - ☐ A. Its strength
   - ☐ B. How it interacts with energy and matter
   - ☐ C. Its 3D aspects
   - ☐ D. What it looks like **[1]**

5. Patents, trademarks and copyright are examples of what?
   - ☐ A. Branding
   - ☐ B. Protection
   - ☐ C. Intellectual property
   - ☐ D. Marketing **[1]**

6. What is affinity diagramming?
   - ☐ A. A diagram that shows relationships
   - ☐ B. A useful tool for product analysis
   - ☐ C. A means of clustering designs that have similar affinities
   - ☐ D. An analysis technique that is a form of brainstorming **[1]**

7. What is semiotics?
   - ☐ A. Types of electronic symbols
   - ☐ B. The study of signs and symbols
   - ☐ C. The means of design communication
   - ☐ D. A type of electronic device **[1]**

8. What are shelved technologies?
   - ☐ A. A structural approach to design
   - ☐ B. Essential technologies of importance
   - ☐ C. Technologies that work with flatpack design
   - ☐ D. When patent inventions are not commercially viable [1]

9. What is a smart material?
   - ☐ A. A material that does not respond to external stimuli
   - ☐ B. A material with one or more properties that can be dramatically altered
   - ☐ C. A material that is used in space
   - ☐ D. Material that has been considered carefully before choosing [1]

10. What is a piezoelectric material?
    - ☐ A. Steel
    - ☐ B. Copper
    - ☐ C. A material that is sensitive to light
    - ☐ D. A material that responds to the application of an applied stress [1]

11. What does ideo-pleasure refer to?
    - ☐ A. The incorporation of personal taste, values, ethics and self-image
    - ☐ B. The psychology of the mind
    - ☐ C. Positive feedback received on a new product
    - ☐ D. The desirability of a product to its end user [1]

12. Which option describes creating radical solutions to problems in competitions with existing products?
    - ☐ A. Innovative design
    - ☐ B. Originality
    - ☐ C. Disruptive innovation
    - ☐ D. Breakthrough design [1]

13. What is triple-bottom-line sustainability?
    - ☐ A. Considering the economics of profit, sustainability and people
    - ☐ B. Focusing on equity, profit and sustainability
    - ☐ C. Considering the economic, environmental and social regions of human activity
    - ☐ D. Concern with planet, people and sustainability [1]

14. What does bottom-up modelling involve?
    - ☐ A. Creating parts before joining them
    - ☐ B. Capturing a new market sector
    - ☐ C. A decline in demand and sales
    - ☐ D. A product gaining acceptance and selling well [1]

15. What is biomimicry?
    - ☐ A. Using biotechnology
    - ☐ B. Transferring a design from nature into design
    - ☐ C. A design which mimics another
    - ☐ D. A biological approach to design [1]

NOTES

16. What is a technology push?

☐ A. When consumers drive change

☐ B. Technology that involves market research

☐ C. When technology adapts to market

☐ D. When innovative technological breakthrough occurs **[1]**

17. What is design for discomfort?

☐ A. Creating a situation that feels uncomfortable or has reduced comfort for limited time

☐ B. Creating a poor design

☐ C. An ergonomic principle

☐ D. Functional and aesthetically appealing design **[1]**

18. What is dematerialization?

☐ A. The selection of material

☐ B. A decline in material quality

☐ C. A reduction in production methods

☐ D. The progressive redirection in the amount of energy and/or material used in the production of a product **[1]**

19. What does circular economy refer to?

☐ A. The concept that: 'What is used, comes around'

☐ B. An economy based upon the use of renewable sources of energy

☐ C. Recycling

☐ D. The global use of a product **[1]**

20. What are percentile ranges?

☐ A. Nominal

☐ B. Ordinal

☐ C. Dividing a sample into 100 equal groups according to a particular variable

☐ D. Multiplying a product cost by the number of users **[1]**

21. What does physiological data refer to?

☐ A. Information gathering focusing on the funding of an individual major organ system

☐ B. Information referring to how people think in certain situations

☐ C. Information based on personal responses to stimuli

☐ D. Information tracking people's moods and attitudes **[1]**

22. What does embodies energy represent?

☐ A. An assessment of all energy misspent manufacturing a product

☐ B. An assessment of all energy not utilized in a product's use

☐ C. An assessment of all energy associated with a product throughout its life

☐ D. All energy tracked and recorded in the product process **[1]**

23. What does cogeneration refer to?

☐ A. Generating two forms of energy from one source (electricity and heat)

☐ B. A theory about design thinking

☐ C. The operation of two generating sources working in parallel

☐ D. A measurement of rate of thinking **[1]**

NOTES

24. What are bottom-up strategies?

☐ A. Multi-nationalist strategies for action

☐ B. Global consortium of agreement for action

☐ C. Strategies introduced by the government

☐ D. Strategies introduced at a regional or local level **[1]**

25. What does a triadic colour scheme involve?

☐ A. Using one or two complementary colours

☐ B. Using a three-colour combination

☐ C. Using colours influenced by light

☐ D. Using a mixture of tertiary colours **[1]**

26. What are digital humans?

☐ A. Real-life users of virtual reality

☐ B. 2-dimensional mannequins

☐ C. Computer-based models used to assist researches in stimulating human biomechanics

☐ D. Robotic users **[1]**

27. What is Finite Element Analysis (FEA)?

☐ A. Testing virtual models under a variety of load conditions

☐ B. Analysing designs to finite degree

☐ C. Specifying quality assurance of models

☐ D. Testing designs to ascertain specific stresses **[1]**

28. What is shape memory?

☐ A. The term used to describe how a material changes once exposed to different temperatures

☐ B. A type of plastic, which once heated cannot be reformed

☐ C. Metals that exhibit pseudo-elasticity due to the rearrangement of their atomic lattice

☐ D. Materials that can regain their status once deformed **[1]**

29. What is pultrusion?

☐ A. Another term for extrusion

☐ B. When material is repeatedly heated and cooled

☐ C. When material to be formed is pulled through a shaped dye

☐ D. When material is slowly cooled **[1]**

30. What is a psychological function?

☐ A. Wants that are driven by fads, fashion and technological needs

☐ B. An emotional attachment to a design

☐ C. A design that features purely in the mind

☐ D. Product testing to seek users' emotional responses **[1]**

31. What is a product family?

☐ A. A range of products focusing on a generation

☐ B. A group of related goods or services

☐ C. Designers who are professionally connected

☐ D. The labelling of similar products **[1]**

NOTES

32. What is additive manufacturing?
- ☐ A. Adding another layer within the manufacturing process
- ☐ B. Technologies used in mass-production methods
- ☐ C. Building physical models by fusing, sintering or polymerizing
- ☐ D. Vacuum forming **[1]**

33. What is value stream mapping?
- ☐ A. Providing a visual aid to map relationships between materials, processes, information and time
- ☐ B. Focusing upon quality assurance of a product
- ☐ C. A way to track cost and time
- ☐ D. An economic tool to seek best value and returns **[1]**

34. What is dominant design?
- ☐ A. In design selection, choosing one design over another
- ☐ B. In design development, focusing upon the best solution
- ☐ C. The emergence of a product that achieves market dominance
- ☐ D. A design that stands out **[1]**

35. What is the purpose of an incremental product?
- ☐ A. Attract customers on own merit
- ☐ B. Frequently make subtle changes to improve
- ☐ C. Keep a trigger product up-to-date
- ☐ D. Engage customers in purchasing add-ons **[1]**

36. What is an eco-phobe?
- ☐ A. Political activism towards environmental change
- ☐ B. Individuals who promote awareness of environmental issues
- ☐ C. People who view the environment as a machine that produces energy and resources to be controlled by man
- ☐ D. Consumers who adopt environmentally friendly practices **[1]**

37. Which of the following is the best sequence of a product life cycle?
- ☐ A. Produce, use, recycle, remake
- ☐ B. Launch, growth, maturity, decline
- ☐ C. Design, manufacture, test, improve
- ☐ D. Decline, redesign, improve, redefine **[1]**

38. What are the characteristics of Lean production?
- ☐ A. Product diversity, multiple product types, short manufacture times
- ☐ B. Volume production, multiple shipments, replaceable workers
- ☐ C. Limited inventories, highly skilled workers, constant improvements
- ☐ D. Reduced lead time, reduced inventory costs, high volume production **[1]**

39. What is biomechanics?
- ☐ A. A type of movement in robotics
- ☐ B. Studying movement in varying scenarios
- ☐ C. The study of mechanical laws relating to the movement of living organisms
- ☐ D. Linkages and mechanisms: how things move and interact **[1]**

40. What does the term continuation refer to?
- ☐ A. Continuous production flow
- ☐ B. The continuity of design ideas
- ☐ C. The method of adopting robotics for continuous production flows
- ☐ D. A technique of tricking the eye into completing objects **[1]**

NOTES

Paper 2: Standard Level/Higher Level

 Set your timer to 1 hour 30 minutes.

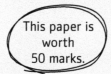 This paper is worth 50 marks.

Section A

Answer **all** the questions in Section A. Write the answers in the space provided.

1. One of the distinctive features of the Galaxy Note 9 is the S Pen. The stylus enables people to write or draw on their phone. This can be useful for those who prefer to make visual notes, such as designers, artists or musicians, and the stylus records the pen's motion, meaning the user can replay the steps taken to create image. It has 4,096 pressure levels, meaning it is as intuitive as pen on paper. The stylus can also be used as a mouse.

   The phone's other features includes:

   - a HDMI port, which allows this to go directly to a screen, eliminating the need for a laptop
   - Bluetooth enabled, allowing users to press a button to take photos or control change of slides during presentation
   - Qualcomm's Snapdragon 845 platform
   - all day prolonged battery charge
   - an intelligent camera system, optimizing colour and light settings, like expose and white settings
   - a water-carbon cooling system, which keeps heat levels down
   - AI enabled technology to suit gamers and to prevent sluggishness
   - ultra-scratch resistant screen with a 1-year guarantee

   The phone's basic model comes with 512 GB storage, and the SD card port allows the option of an additional 512 GB storage. It is available in a few monochrome metal shades with matching stylus.

   Samsung is currently the largest manufacturer of mobile phones in the world. However, with its price tag of 1,000 USD, this model is not going to be affordable to everybody.

   Figure 1: A stylus being used on a smartphone

NOTES

(a) (i) Describe one unique feature of the Note 9. **[2]**

....

....

(ii) Outline one reason why a water-cooling system is incorporated into the phone. **[2]**

....

....

....

....

(b) (i) Outline one advantage of the Bluetooth-enabled technology. **[2]**

....

....

....

....

(ii) Describe how the Note 9 is an example of innovation and design. **[2]**

....

....

....

....

(c) (i) Outline one reason why the Note 9 might not be chosen by everybody. **[2]**

....

....

....

....

(ii) Explain how the unique features of the Note 9 differentiate this product from other competitors. **[3]**

....

....

....

....

....

(d) (i) Describe how the Note 9 meets the criteria for converging technology. **[2]**

....

....

....

....

NOTES

(ii) Outline one advantage of converging technologies for the customer. **[2]**

....

....

....

(e) SAR (Specific Absorption Rates) measure the rate of radiation on human body tissue. The tables below show head SAR (Specific Absorption Rates) for mobile phones. The FCC permits public exposure from a cellular telephone to be no higher than 1.6 watts of energy absorbed per kilogram of body weight. ALL phone radiation can heat human body tissue.

Figure 2: List of smartphones with levels of emitted radiation

Manufacturer	Model	SAR value (W/kg)
Samsung	Note 9 Exynos	0.381
Samsung	Galaxy S9	0.29
LG	V40 thinQ	0.318
Razer Inc	Razer Phone	0.35
LG	G7 thinQ	0.244
Samsung	Galaxy S6	0.382
Motorola	Moto g6 plus	0.44
Nokia	8	0.711
HTC	Google Pixel	1.34
Apple	iPhone XS	1.19
OnePlus	OnePlus X	1.018

(Figures from Federal Communications Commission, www.fcc.gov/oet/ea/fccid)

(i) Identify which mobile phone has the lowest SAR rating and which has the highest SAR rating. **[2]**

....

....

....

....

(ii) Outline how SAR data ratings are important for the manufacturer. **[2]**

....

....

....

....

(iii) Outline why SAR data ratings are important for the consumer. **[2]**

....

....

....

....

(iv) Outline the role of the designer in reducing the SAR rating of a mobile phone. [2]

....

....

....

....

2. Explain how the use of motion capture software assists designers in choosing materials. [2]

....

....

....

....

....

3. State **three** reasons why spider silk is considered to be the strongest of all fibres. [3]

....

....

....

....

....

NOTES

Section B

Answer **only one** question from Section B. Write the answers in the space provided.

4. Hyundai have developed a prototype quadrupedal called the 'Elevate'. It uses the technology of electric cars and advanced robotics, and can clamber over uneven rubble whilst keeping the passengers steady or can be controlled remotely. It relies on electric actuator technology. The design allows six movements in any direction: horizontal hip, vertical hip, ankle, knee, wheel, and steering. The legs are designed to be retractable, meaning they can be folded, allowing the Elevate to be driven as a vehicle, and it can climb over walls up to 5 foot high. It has two walking modes: reptilian (with legs outreached) and mammalian (legs front and back). The cockpit has four-door access, allowing quick entry and exits.

It is intended for use in emergency response but could be used in a number of extreme situations, such as traversing a newly discovered planet, snow, or earthquake sites for humanitarian aid.

Figure 3: Elevate from Hyundai combines four legs and four wheels

(a) Outline how this is a good example of concept modelling. **[2]**

(b) (i) Explain how Elevate incorporates human factors in its concept rationale. **[3]**

(ii) Discuss how the unique robotic leg system allows manoeuvrability. **[3]**

NOTES

(c) (i) Discuss one reason why an established company such as Hyundai is
interested in a vehicle different from the mainstream. [3]

....

....

....

....

....

....

(ii) Elevate is currently at the concept modelling prototype stage to test
the appetite of the market to buy. Explain how the different aspects
of Elevate's design could appeal to three different target markets: the
military, the space industry and humanitarian organizations. [9]

....

....

....

....

....

....

....

....

....

....

....

....

....

....

....

....

....

....

....

....

....

....

....

NOTES

NOTES

5. Figure 4 shows a person wingsuiting (skydiving). A wingsuit is a specially designed suit made to add surface area to the human body in order to create a significant increase in lift. The person wingsuiting normally carries a parachute too.

A wingsuit can have three individual ram-air wings attached: one between the legs and one under each arm. It works by utilizing the resistance of the air: air is pushed through inlets in the suit to inflate membranes, which helps maintain the airfoil as semirigid. Another type of wingsuit works on a similar principle, but instead of three wings it is made up of one big wing.

Ripstop nylon is usually used for the main surface of a wingsuit, but other various materials reinforce the leading edge, reduce drag and provide comfort.

Figure 4: A wingsuit in action

Figure 5: Different wingsuit movements

(a) (i) Outline the meaning of the phrase 'specially designed suit' in this context. [2]

(ii) Outline why ripstop nylon is one of the main materials used. **[2]**

(b) (i) List two design features you would expect to be thoroughly tested to ensure the health and safety of the wingsuit user. **[2]**

(ii) Originally the wing was made using a combination of materials, including whale bone. Describe how you think the whale bone would have been incorporated. **[2]**

(iii) Explain how the airfoil shape has been constructed. **[3]**

(c) Usability is how well a product can effectively and efficiently be used. Explain the usefulness, effectiveness and learnability of the wingsuit in relation to the user. **[9]**

NOTES

6. The iconic London red telephone box was created by Sir Giles Gilbert Scott for a design competition in 1924. The aim was to create a standardised design that would be accepted by the London boroughs. Originally prototyped in plywood, it was introduced to London in 1926.

There have been several series and different models of telephone boxes. The K6 (kiosk number six) was introduced in 1935 to commemorate King George V's silver jubilee. It stands at 8 feet 3 inches (2.51 metres) tall and is 3 feet wide. It weighs 13.5 cwt (0.69 tonnes) and was the first design to have a glazing pattern of six glass panels on three sides. The material is cast iron (bolted together) and teak doors. It has Serif lettering upon opaque glass and a pediment that carries a moulded Royal crown. Now they are usually painted 'currant red', which is defined by the British Standard colour chart reference as BS381C-Red539.

Between 1935 and 1968, 60,000 of K6 telephone boxes were introduced. They are featured in pop culture such as Adele's 'Hello' music video and the front cover of One Direction's *Take Me Home* album. They can also be found all over the world.

Figure 6: a K6 telephone box

(a) Outline one distinctive design feature of the K6 telephone box. **[2]**

....

....

....

....

(b) Outline one way that the design of the K6 benefits portability. **[2]**

....

....

....

....

....

NOTES

(c) Describe the method of manufacture of the K6. [4]

....
....
....
....
....
....
....

(d) Discuss why teak might have been used for the door. [3]

....
....
....
....
....

(e) Explain three reasons why the K6 design may be considered a
classic design. [9]

....
....
....
....
....
....
....
....
....
....
....
....
....
....
....
....

Paper 3: Higher Level

Set your timer to 1 hour 30 minutes.

This paper is worth 40 marks.

Section A

Answer **all** the questions given. Write the answers in the space provided.

Use of calculators is allowed.

1. The TAP keyboard/mouse won the prestigious Red Dot award for Product Design in 2019. It offers users an innovative alternative to using a keyboard and mouse. Instead, these functions are offered from a single device worn on the user's hand like five connected rings. It can be used with tablets and smartphones, as well as with computers. It has a fairly high price tag of $199 (USD).

    Users of the TAP keyboard/mouse need to be very familiar with QWERTY finger patterns and character mapping. The designers have produced a training app called TAP Genius, which is available on iOS. This has been produced to help make the anthropometric design of the finger combinations easier to use.

    Other features include:

    *   Wireless Bluetooth connectivity
    *   Adjustable ring sizes
    *   Portable charging case
    *   Light weight (45 g)
    *   Five 3-axis accelerometer sensors
    *   8-hour battery life
    *   64-hour case battery life

    Figure 1: TAP keyboard/mouse has won a Red Dot award: Product Design 2019. Displayed on hand and in the charging case.

    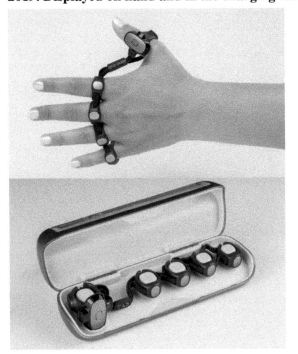

NOTES

(a) Outline two ways that the TAP keyboard/mouse may be considered a good example of a user-centred design. [4]

....

....

....

....

....

(b) Outline one reason why users might be dismissive of this product as opposed to a conventional keyboard. [2]

....

....

....

....

....

(c) Explain three ways that the TAP keyboard/mouse designers have specifically considered the user's requirements when creating this new method of interacting with other devices. [6]

....

....

....

....

....

....

....

....

....

....

....

2. **Figure 2: The 2018 Yamaha NIKEN**

NIKEN is a three-wheeler with a liquid-cooled three-cylinder engine. It uses Leaning Multi-Wheel (LMW) technology controlled by Computer Integrated Manufacturing (CIM) and a unique steering geometry system, which provides separate steering and lean axles. It allows wheels which are tied to an axle to track independently and safely when turning. The inner wheel follows a smaller radius than the outer to prevent slipping and/or scrubbing.

Having three wheels provides a greater degree of stability; especially during turns on windy roads, and solid contact with the ground is provided by a strong undercarriage. It also has a powerful shoulder area and slim tank, which allows knee grip combinations, creating a sense of greater control and further stability. It looks sporty and athletic and is a unique riding experience.

The price is slightly higher than a conventional two-wheeler; it is selling well in Europe. It appeals to regular commuters, as it has the power to match a supercar, the feeling of a superbike, but is also safer.

Yamaha epitomizes the benefits of Lean Production based upon principles of Kaizen. NIKEN won the 'Best of the Best' award in the 2019 Red Dot Product Design competition.

(a) Describe how Yamaha has created a distinctive brand identity. **[2]**

....

....

....

....

(b) Explain how Yamaha uses market segmentation as part of its product development strategy. **[3]**

....

....

....

....

....

(c) Discuss how CIM might be useful for Yamaha's efficiency. **[3]**

....

....

....

....

....

....

....

NOTES

Section B

3. Read the case study. Answer the following question.

Figure 3: An example of a flying car

An all-electric flying-car concept has been launched by Pop.Up Next, via collaboration with Audi, Airbus and Italdesign. The prototype was shown at a fair in Amsterdam. This is an example of a hybrid-innovative product, merging self-driving cars and passenger drones.

The innovative design is made of three separate modules: passengers sit in a two-seat capsule and a four-rotor drone is put together through a detachable pod. The drone flies autonomously, leading to some people arguing that this is a step towards flying taxis. This could make people who are unable to drive more mobile and utilise airspace to help reduce traffic on roads, particularly in congested areas like cities.

(a) Describe what the name Pop.Up Next suggest about the corporate strategy that Airbus and Audi are adopting.   **[2]**

....

....

....

....

....

....

(b) State one way in which the designs mark an important milestone in terms of defining new markets sectors and segments.   **[1]**

....

....

....

....

....

....

....

NOTES

(c) Describe how Audi and Airbus have enhanced their branding. **[2]**

....
....
....
....
....

(d) Explain why Pop.Up Next is a good example of innovation in the market.

[6]

....
....
....
....
....
....
....
....
....
....

(e) Explain three reasons why Pop.Up Next appeared at the Turin Motor Show and Amsterdam Drone week as part of their marketing strategy. **[9]**

....
....
....
....
....
....
....
....
....
....
....
....
....
....
....
....

NOTES

Answers

Set A
Standard Level: Paper 1

Question No.	Answer	Question No.	Answer
1	D	16	C
2	A	17	B
3	C	18	A
4	D	19	A
5	A	20	C
6	B	21	C
7	C	22	C
8	A	23	A
9	A	24	B
10	C	25	D
11	D	26	B
12	B	27	B
13	B	28	C
14	A	29	D
15	C	30	A

Higher Level: Paper 1

Question No.	Answer	Question No.	Answer
1	D	21	C
2	A	22	A
3	C	23	D
4	C	24	C
5	D	25	B
6	B	26	C
7	C	27	B
8	B	28	B
9	B	29	D
10	D	30	C
11	D	31	B
12	A	32	B
13	B	33	B
14	D	34	A
15	C	35	D
16	B	36	C
17	C	37	A
18	C	38	B
19	C	39	D
20	D	40	C

Set A: Standard and Higher Level: Paper 2

Section A

1. (a) (i) • Invention and innovation are a result of a need to solve
    or simplify a problem. When the innovative idea helps
    simplify the problem then the innovation is successful
    • Hence an innovation requires the designer to address the
    current trends in the market and identify the needs of the
    users with an existing product
    • The outcome of understanding the user views is a more
    successful innovation: improved usability, quality and
    user-friendliness
    Award [1] each for any two correct responses from above.
    Accept any other reasonable suggestion.   **[Max 2]**

(ii) • Ethically considering the responsibility to the safety
    of the user, whether the product is being used, stored
    or charged
    • Choosing the manufacturing processes which are
    environmentally friendly
    • The product life-cycle consequences need to be analysed
    • Manufacturing standards set need to be acceptable both
    locally and internationally
    • Privacy and rights to other company's property should not
    be invaded
    • The affordability of costs needs to be analysed
    • Provision of the company's operational infrastructure,
    e.g. information technology, policies, processes or data
    • Effect on the natural environment caused due to the
    development and use of the product
    • Considerations to the loss or creation of jobs for the
    community
    Award [1] for the ethical consideration and [1] for the
    reason given in context to Toyota. Accept any other
    reasonable suggestion.   **[Max 2]**

(b) • Even though old products remain functional, sometimes
    consumer willingness to accept and use new innovative
    products may be a result of new products becoming simpler
    to use and user-friendly
    • Newer products have the capability of providing a better
    facility, more durability and a better warranty/guarantee
    • Newer products may be looked at as having an iconic status
    in society
    • A willingness of users to adapt current trends or fashions
    provide inspiration for designers in the development of
    new products
    • It is necessary for designers to constantly make improvements
    in existing designs in order to stay a step ahead of the
    competitors so that they don't lose market share and
    brand image
    • Considering the advancements in environmental aspects may
    inspire innovative redesigning of older products
    Accept any four responses from above. Award [1]
    for each correct response. Accept any other reasonable
    suggestion.   **[Max 4]**

(c) • Usage of sustainable materials encourages the development
    of innovative products by crossing the barriers to current
    design processes and options
    • The social pressure for the use of eco-friendly products may
    encourage designers to explore sustainable alternatives
    • The iterative nature of the design process provides
    designers opportunities to investigate other possible
    sustainable materials thereby designing the existing
    designed solutions
    • The process of designing innovative products consists of
    investigating, examining and studying the potentials of using
    sustainable materials
    Accept any three responses from above. Award [1] for
    each each correct response. Accept any other reasonable
    suggestion.   **[Max 3]**

(d) • Responsibility to adhere to the intellectual property of Toyota
    mobility solutions
    • Ensuring the total safety of the users
    • Studying the consequences of injuries caused to the users
    while using the solutions
    • Considering the effect of damage to a third party or property
    • Policies and insurance necessities for the third-party materials
    • Responsibilities pertaining to the licensing of any
    requirements
    • Adhering to local and international manufacturing standards
    • Accountabilities for ownership in the operation of solutions
    • Intervention in terms of emergency services required
    • Documentation in terms of policies and product warranty
    Accept any three responses from above. Award [1] for each correct
    response. Accept any other reasonable suggestion.   **[Max 3]**

(e) (i) • Anthropometrics
 • Physiological factors
 • Psychological factors
 Award [1] for each correct response. **[Max 3]**

   (ii) • The human factors of the two chairs include the ergonomic as well as the anthropometric factors significant to their use
 • The office chair is expected to be used for a longer duration than a bar stool. Hence, it is important to give the ability of adjustment for height and comfort in terms of the correct back/lumbar support for the user
 • Both the chairs will be located in an area where aesthetics are important. However, the aesthetics of the bar chair in a social setting will have a greater impact compared to the office chair
 • In terms of function, the bar stool should be more stable compared to an office chair. Office chairs have wheels for better movability
 • Ergonomic consideration needs to be given to both the chairs as correct height will ensure comfort. The office chair also has a suitable backrest and armrest
 Accept any three responses. Award [1] for each correct response. Accept any other reasonable suggestion. **[Max 3]**

2. (a) • While developing a new product, the designer should ensure that it meets the intended purpose of the product. It is important to take into consideration first the product's functional requirements rather than making it aesthetically appealing, although this also determines its success in the marketplace
 • An example could be a sports water bottle design, which must be lightweight, easy to move and leak-proof. These factors are important more than the form and aesthetics
 Award [1] for a correct response. Award [1] for an explanation. **[Max 2]**

(b) • Conceptual sketching allows a designer to visualize and express their ideas easily
 • They are quick to draw, which helps a designer to progress with their design ideas and their understanding of the design problem
 • These ideas can be easily expressed in real time, including complex ideas
 • Computer-based designs may not allow an immediate real-time response. A conceptual sketch may help the design team and aid the quality of the communication situation
 Accept any three responses. Award [1] for each correct response. Accept any other reasonable suggestion. **[Max 3]**

3. • Designers have access to various technologies in daily work practices, but this can have both positive and negative impacts
 • The positive impact will be that the CAD modelling technology which is used allows designers to electronically share their design ideas with the design team and the stakeholders anywhere in the world. This leads to better collaboration and aids the product's development process
 • The negative impact is the high initial installation costs incurred in establishing such technologies and staff training adds to the total cost of the process
 Accept any two responses. Award [1] for each correct response. Accept any other reasonable suggestion. **[Max 2]**

4. Aesthetics
 • increase the interest of the consumers in the product
 • grab the attention of consumers towards the product
 • make products likeable with features like texture, colour, shape and size
 • have a vital role in online shopping
 Accept any three responses. Award [1] for each correct response. Accept any other reasonable suggestion. **[Max 3]**

Section B

5. (a) • Technology with two or more distinct technologies adapted into a single product. This is to offer greater accessibility, productivity and new features that did not previously exist in older products

• It also aids in reducing the material dependence and energy required in the manufacturing of the new product
 Award [2] for a correct response and explanation. **[Max 2]**

(b) • Smartphones
 • Electric vehicles
 • Fitness bands
 • Laptops
 • Wearable technologies, e.g. smart clothing
 • Scanners
 • Printers
 Accept any three responses from above. Award [1] for each correct response. **[Max 3]**

(c) • Enhanced accessibility to communicate long-distance video conferencing
 • Applications in medical activities, such as diagnosing the patients faster
 • The features of compact designing: making one product instead of two solves the problem of space saving
 • Complex to learn different technologies. It is better to learn it all in one product, thereby simplifying the operational use
 • The process of manufacturing the product is economical Also maintenance cost is less compared to repairing different products
 Award [2] each for any three requirements in the society with explanation of the requirement. **[Max 6]**

(d) • Initial cost incurred to buy and maintain a particular technology
 • Discrimination of the users appropriate to the age, gender, religious or cultural beliefs
 • Consumer pressures towards green designs and sustainability issues
 • Newer technologies can bring better employment opportunities (for new skilled and unskilled jobs), e.g. in the fields of CAD, CAM and ATMs
 • Social dependence through technological contact, e.g. SMS, Facebook, Skype and Twitter
 • A loss to cultural identities due to globalisation and westernisation
 Award [3] for each of three distinct points of social issues and analysis of each issue. **[Max 9]**

6. (a) • Style (fashion) obsolescence
 • Functional obsolescence
 • Technological obsolescence
 Award [1] each for any of the two features of planned obsolescence. **[Max 2]**

(b) • To ensure the replacement of an existing product with a newly improved product
 • To escalate the sales and profits of the company
 • To provide openings for new versions of the products
 • To integrate emerging technologies with the products
 Award [1] for each of the three points from above. Do not accept if a response is not clear. **[Max 3]**

(c) **Advantages:**
 • Consumers get introduced to new improved technologies when new products are launched
 • Accessible to the latest fashion trends in the global community
 • As a result of volume sales, the company benefits from the profits incurred
 • An overall rise in the country's economies
 • Employment opportunities for native people

Disadvantages:
 • A continuous necessity for replacement and related inconvenience
 • Inability to repair or replace the product even if consumers are satisfied
 • Disconcert within technophobes for a new product or technology
 • Increase independence on the use of the materials and energy required for manufacturing new products
 Award [1] for each of three advantages of planned obsolescence. Award [1] for each of three disadvantages. Do not accept if the response is not clear. **[Max 6]**

(d) **Society**: Allows users to use emerging technologies; Options to choose a product from the marketplace based on the user's choice and needs; When a new technology supersedes and existing technology, the existing technology falls out of use and is no longer incorporated into new products. Consumers instead are forced to opt for and benefit from the newer, more efficient technology in products.

Environment: Allows green materials as an alternative in the production of new products, thereby increasing the recyclability in the environment; By manufacturing new products, the process leads to increased waste products which are often dumped; New inventions/technologies may use less energy in manufacturing and have better biodegradable capabilities.

Design process: New designs may lead to replacing obsolete production processes; Newer versions may ensure additional safety factors; Increases the scope for innovation.

Award [3] for each of the three distinct points of effects of planned obsolescence with explanation each point. **[Max 9]**

7. (a) • Green design refers to designs having reduced consequences on the environment during its entire product life cycle
   • More precisely, this means decreasing environmental impacts linked with its product design, material extraction, production, use, maintenance and end-of-life discarding

Award [2] for any of the above correct responses. **[Max 2]**

(b) • Minimizing of poisonous diffusion into the environment
   • Extending the products durability and robustness
   • Expanding sustainable use of eco-friendly resources
   • Enhancing the facilities of goods and services
   • Decreasing the amount of material and energy required in providing goods and services
   • Attaining accreditation in qualifying to do business in some fields

Award [1] for each of three design objectives from above. **[Max 3]**

(c) • The use of eco-friendly materials extends the difficulties or limitations of current design decisions or solutions
   • The social recognition of eco-friendly materials inspires designers to discover alternatives in the innovative design solutions that use these technologies
   • The cyclical nature of the design activity allows designers to explore eco-friendly materials which lead to developing an existing designed solution
   • The idea of testing the possibilities of using eco-friendly materials further enhances the development of design ideas that encompassing the use of innovative technologies

Award [2] for each of three points from above with an explanation of each. **[Max 6]**

(d) • Designers need to consider designing products with a sustainable approach due to the decreasing supply of traditional resources such as fossil, metals and mineral ores. Thereby green products are being developed that allow designers to consider a wider variety of materials for the production of design solutions.
   • For achieving this, the use of alternative solutions should be encouraged. For example, an alternative decomposable option to plastic such as 'Biopak', which is an ecological form of packaging. By using such materials, the problem of waste elimination is reduced at the end of the user's side.
   • With an increase in pressure from consumers to use green products, this is an important consideration for the designer. So if a designer decides to use materials like Biopak in the packing of the products, then it will appeal to more users.
   • If a designer achieves greater sales through the design of such products, this, in turn, will increase the profits for the company commissioning the designer.
   • This increase will also lead to ethical consumerism within the consumers.
   • However, the real challenge lies in the cost of research and development incurred by the designers in the process and the companies need to tackle this.
   • A lot of dedication and time is required to develop sustainable products.
   • There is no fixed scale to the implementation and development of green products; it may take months or years to improve and it is the necessity of the company to remain financially sound during that time.

• The research and development required in the process are sometimes out of reach for several designers and so they follow the traditional design practices and depend on the non-renewable resources for production.
• In the introduction stage of a product into a marketplace, sustainable products are usually more expensive in comparison with traditional products.
• It is the responsibility of the designers to consider the developments in materials and the cost-effectiveness in the long run. This will help change the universal demands and design trends, which can overcome the challenges of the temporary costs of building sustainable products.

Award [3] for each of the three distinct points with an explanation of opportunities and or challenges. **[Max 9]**

Set A: Higher Level: Paper 3

Section A

1. (a) • Designers help sustainable development across different contexts. A systematic method is required in all design stages to satisfy all the stakeholders involved.
   • In developing sustainable products, designers must ensure the equilibrium between aesthetic, financial, social, cultural, energy, material, health and usability concerns of the users.

Award [1] for each of the two distinct points. Do not accept if a response is not clear. **[Max 2]**

(b) • Sustainable innovation enables the usage of sustainable solutions in the marketplace. It produces both bottom-line and top-line returns to the companies investing in it; it develops products and systems that are eco-friendly, and reduces the costs by reducing the resources required to make the product.
   • Designers need to critically adhere to the compliance with government regulation as a chance for sustainable innovation.

Award [1] for each of the two distinct points. Do not accept only one response. **[Max 2]**

(c) • Triple bottom line sustainability does not only focus on the financial profits of a company or product but also the environmental and social benefit it can get
   • Companies that adapt TBL sustainability can make substantial positive effects on the lives of people and the ecosystem by altering the impact of their business activities

Award [1] for each of the two distinct points. Do not accept only one response. **[Max 2]**

(d) • **Cyclic:** Products should mandatorily be part of the recycling system, by natural methods such as composting or recycling.
   • **Solar:** An amount of energy required to manufacture and use the product should originate from renewable energy sources in any of the forms.
   • **Safe:** During the production, products should not produce toxic by-products nor contain any hazardous contents.
   • **Efficient:** Designs should be developed considering only one-tenth of the materials and energy previously used. Designs that provide multiple functions or converging technologies reduce the impact of multiple products.
   • **Social:** Safe health-and-safety practices should be observed during the production and post-production. It should also follow fair trade principles.

Award [1] each for any of the four correct responses from above. **[Max 4]**

2. (a) • User-centred design (UCD) is a method of designing products considering the needs, wants and limitations of the end user at every stage of the design cycle
   • In designing for UCD, it is fundamental to have a deep understanding of the users, task and the environment in which the product shall be used

Award [1] for each of the correct responses. Do not accept if a response is not clear. **[Max 2]**

(b) • Categorization of users based on factors such as age, gender and physical health condition
   • The practice of using personae, secondary personae and anti-personae during user research
   • Use case, making a formal written report of the style in which the user will interact with the product
   • Studying the methods of extremes
   • Observations

- Interviews
- Focus groups
- Affinity diagramming

Award [1] each for any of the correct responses. Do not accept if a response is not clear. **[Max 2]**

(c) • Inclusive design is the design of products and environments which can be utilisable by anyone, without the need for specialised adaptation. Its objective is to simplify life for everybody by creating products with little cost or no cost.
- It may involve those who are pregnant, elderly, disabled or injured.

Award [1] for each of the correct responses. Do not accept if a response is not clear. **[Max 2]**

(d) • **Research:** Design problems relating to the requirements of users, task and the environment are explored. This is done with a multi-disciplinary team consisting of ethnographers, anthropologists and psychologists.
- **Concept:** Initial ideas developed for the problem are put forward. This may include concept modelling, evaluations, feedback from the users and feeding back this input into the design cycle. A multi-disciplinary team of various engineers, psychologists and engineers work together closely.
- **Design:** Development of feasible ideas, prototyping and mock-ups is made to monitor the performance against the usability requirements of the products.
- **Implementation:** Users' psychological and physiological experience using the product is tested and evaluated. The evaluation is fed back into the design cycle.
- **Launch:** The final product is launched into the market. Evaluation is still carried out.

Award [1] for each of the correct responses with a correct explanation. **[Max 4]**

Section B

3. (a) • A pioneering strategy involves an innovative development in a product or service offered by a company. It enables manufacturers to have a competitive advantage in being first in a market with a product or service.
- This approach incurs a lot of research and development of the existing market and market pioneers are required to consider this.

Award [1] for each of the correct responses. Do not accept if a response is not clear. **[Max 2]**

(b) • By registering a trademark, the company is provided with a variety of protection opportunities. It indicates to other companies their authorized rights to entirely claim the rights of promoting the registered products.
- This can lead to legal action taken against companies who use it without the permission or a licence from the registrar.

Award [1] for each of the correct responses. **[Max 2]**

(c) • Eco-warriors
- Eco-champions
- Eco-fans
- Eco-phobes

Award [1] for each of the correct responses. Do not accept only 1 response. **[Max 2]**

(d) • CSR is a business strategy. It states the company's strategic approach for the future.
- It is a self-assessment to understand the current situation and plan policies and procedures to accomplish pre-set goals by the company.
- The goals may involve environmental or financial benefits to the company. It is the duty of every business to make a profit and also to adapt the CSR principles and practices.
- These activities suggest improving society without harming the environment.
- Using CSR sustainable, eco-friendly practices can reduce the cost and waste generated by the production practices of the company. By undertaking such activities, it helps to boost the overall public approval ratings of the company.

Award [1] for each of the correct responses. Do not accept if a response is not clear. **[Max 5]**

(e) • Cost plus strategy is a method which adds a small standard percentage of profit over the cost of producing the product. It is important to assess the fixed and variable costs in this particular pricing method.

- Demand pricing is a method based on the consumer's opinion of the product value in the marketplace. Branding allows manufacturers to charge the product at a premium. There are possibilities of rarity or scarcity of the demands in the market of such marketing styles. Products that carry an innovative feature can also facilitate premium prices.
- Competitor-based pricing is a method based on the common market rate or the 'ongoing rate' of similar products charged by competing companies. Companies use the technique of offering an incentive to users if they can find the same product at a lower rate than they have charged, thus engaging them in the current market-price investigations.
- Product-line pricing is a strategy used to increase profits. Companies offer a range of upgrades or improvements to the primary product. Automobiles are good examples of product-line pricing, where the organization offers a variety of add-ons to improve the sales. The objective is to maximize profits: the more options chosen means the more the customer will agree to pay.
- Psychological pricing is a method based on a price that appears better. For example, $5.99 per kilogram looks significantly cheaper than $6.00 per kilogram. This is why many prices end with '.99' or '.98' as it gives users the impression of them paying less. Consumers read the price from left to right, which means they focus primarily on the dollar amounts. This means that companies can charge the higher amounts for a product while still offering a lower psychological price perception to the consumers.

Award [3] for each of the strategies with a correct explanation. **[Max 9]**

Set B

Standard Level: Paper 1

Question No.	Answer	Question No.	Answer
1	B	16	A
2	D	17	C
3	B	18	A
4	B	19	A
5	B	20	D
6	A	21	B
7	B	22	C
8	D	23	B
9	B	24	B
10	B	25	A
11	B	26	A
12	B	27	C
13	B	28	B
14	B	29	B
15	C	30	B

Higher Level: Paper 1

Question No.	Answer	Question No.	Answer
1	C	21	C
2	B	22	B
3	B	23	B
4	D	24	B
5	C	25	A
6	B	26	D
7	A	27	B
8	B	28	B
9	C	29	B
10	B	30	C
11	B	31	C
12	A	32	B
13	B	33	B
14	A	34	C
15	B	35	C
16	A	36	B
17	A	37	C
18	C	38	B
19	A	39	B
20	B	40	D

Set B: Standard and Higher Level: Paper 2

Section A

1. (a) (i) • 5th–95th percentile taking into consideration the adults (also accept 2.5th–97.5th)
        Award [1] for the correct response from above for the correct percentile range. **[Max 1]**

    (ii) • The anthropometric data relating to 50th percentile adult hand size
            – to be comfortable to grip and the correct size for a hand
        • Texture of the material
            – in relation to the grip/not slippery/comfortable
        • The shape of the handlebars
            – in relation to the grip/comfortable for hands/easy to hold
        Award [1] for any of the correct responses from above and award [1] for an explanation on ergonomic consideration. **[Max 2]**

    (b) (i) • Transparent
        • Resistant to chemicals and moisture from the surrounding environment
        • Easy to clean
        • Easy to mould in any complex shape
        • Cheap
        Award [1] each for any two of the correct responses from above. Do not accept if a response is not clear. **[Max 2]**

    (ii) • Safer than glass even if it is damaged
        • Density is less and hence it is easier/lighter to carry
        • Durability is high as it does not break easily
        • Cheaper and easy to manufacture
        • Choice in choosing plastics is available as a variety of plastic types exist
        Award [1] each for any two of the correct responses from above. **[Max 2]**

    (c) (i) • Decisions regarding the scope of LCA assessment at every step in the design cycle are taken
        • Which will further have impact on the environmental aspect of the matrix
        Award [2] for the correct responses from above. Do not accept if a response is not clear. **[Max 2]**

    (ii) • Designers can use the matrix to assess the impact of decisions taken at the stages of the design cycle
        • On the following product life cycle
        • And the environment
        Award [3] for the correct responses from above. Do not accept if a response is not clear. **[Max 3]**

    (d) (i) • Hot gas
        • Friction welding
        • Ultrasonic welding
        • Laser welding
        Award [1] for any of the correct responses from above. Do not accept if a response is not clear. **[Max 1]**

    (ii) • Does not allow disassembly of the product
        • Difficulty in repair and maintenance
        • Hence products are forced to be discarded after a short product life cycle
        Award [2] for points from the correct responses from above. **[Max 2]**

    (e) (i) • Solar
        • Wind
        • Biomass
        • Wave
        • Tidal
        • Hydro-electric
        • Geothermal
        Award [1] each for any of the two correct responses from above. **[Max 2]**

    (ii) • High cost of installation initially
        • Little economy of scale
        • The supply may be unreliable as energy source may be inconsistent, depending on location and season or weather
        • The amount of energy produced does not meet the required demand, hence low energy density

        • Fossil fuels are usually much cheaper than renewable resources, e.g. coal is an abundant resource and is also readily available
        • Tradition plays an important role, as fossil fuels have been used for centuries and the technology is also well understood
        Award [1] each for any three of the correct responses above. **[Max 3]**

2. (a) (i) • Image
        • Dominant design
        • Iconic
        • Recognisable
        • Timeless
        • Omnipresent
        Award [1] each for any of the two correct responses from above. **[Max 2]**

    (ii) • The various models of each Stratocaster series have specific functions
        • Meaning that the form of the Stratocaster series dictates its purpose
        • The function of each miniature feature is designed first
        • The form of a guitar is designed around the size of the features
        • The shape or the form of a guitar is restrained and is simple
        • But primarily designed to accommodate a complex set of controls separately within
        Award [1] each for a correct response and [1] for a correct description. **[Max 2]**

3. To:
    • Test the comfort/texture/size/shape/grip
    • Test the position of the steering/position of the button
    • Collect data/get authentic feedback from the potential users
        – which will help in iterating/developing the shape/improve the ergonomics in the car
    Award [3] for the reason of using modelling technique with an explanation. **[Max 3]**

4. • Cradle to cradle encourages recyclability of a product/system (do not accept recycle or reuse) by reducing the waste from going in the landfill
    • It provides a more sustainable or eco-friendly approach
    • Cradle to cradle encourages waste eradication by increasing recyclability, which is a circular strategy
    • Cradle to grave takes into account the total environmental effects of a product from pre-production to disposal, which is a linear strategy
    • Cradle to cradle decreases the effect on resources
    Award [1] each for any of the three correct responses from above. **[Max 3]**

Section B

5. (a) 3D printing:
        • Can create complicated figures
        • Can make components of high accuracy and precision
        • Process can be faster than conventional methods of manufacturing
        • Minimises waste created in the production
        • Can be created as a solo component
        • Reduces the number of overall processes necessary
        • Flexible to make changes to/customise the product
        Award [1] each for the two correct responses from above. Do not accept if a response is not clear. **[Max 2]**

    (b) • High thermal resistance
            – Will not be damaged by playing/being left in the sun
        • Lightweight
            – Easy for children to carry around
        • Manufacturing can be done in high volumes with high precision and low cost
            – Can meet demand and sell to consumers cheaply
        • Plastic can be remoulded and recycled on application of heat
            – Reduce wastage/reuse defective products
        • Maintains its shape thus reducing the potential of deformation
            – Will not be easily damaged by children
        • Oxidisation and corrosion resistance
            – Long lasting/years of use for children
        • Makes it more durable and easier to maintain

Award [1] each for two correct reasons for using thermoplastic.
And award [1] giving an explanation of the same. **[Max 3]**

(c) Cost:
- Injection moulding is a mass-production process, also called continuous flow method of production
- This means the units cost per product can be kept low
- This benefits the overall economy of scale
- Injection moulding creates a precise finishing to the surface of the product
- Thus minimising the need for additional finishing techniques like dip coating/painting/galvanising, etc.
- It also saves the manufacturing time and cost for labour

Waste:
- The leftover plastic created during the injection moulding process can be reheated and restored into the moulding process
- Thus reducing the need for additional raw materials for the production
- The injection moulding can manufacture accurate parts, which means high precision and less mistakes in production, thus less waste generated during production.

Award [1] for each of the distinct responses in an explanation of cost incurred in the injection moulding process [3 max] and waste incurred in the injection moulding process.
Award [1] each for three reasons for cost reduction and award [1] each for three reasons for waste reduction with the use of injection moulding. **[Max 6]**

(d) **Consumers**
- Increasing public awareness of global environmental issues has put pressure on corporations and governments through purchasing and voting power of consumers
- Social pressure for the use of environmentally friendly materials in products
- Increasing consumer demand for toys created in an environmentally friendly and sustainable way
- Consumer pressure for use of recyclability packaging
- Support for production methods that do not have an undesirable effect on employees

Legislation
- Governments may offer incentives to companies who adopt eco-friendly practices
- Compulsory labelling of materials acts as an incentive for companies to produce recyclable packaging
- Companies may be discouraged by penalities imposed by them not adopting eco-friendly practices
- Companies will need to ensure that their manufacturers are operating production units in an eco-friendly manner which will make them more conscious
- The designers would need to comply with government regulations on waste

Environmental concerns:
- Commitment to using sustainable resources
- Encouraging social responsibility towards the community
- Eco-friendly practices can reduce the cost and waste generated by the production practices of the company
- Recyclability of a product/system by ensure the waste doesn't end up in landfill

Award [1] each for identifying three drivers for green design and [1] for an explanation of each identified driver. **[Max 9]**

6. (a)
- Evolution in the technology used in conventional buses
- Efficiency is higher than conventional buses
- Reduced noise levels in comparison to gas, diesel engines
- Provides a market opportunity for the introduction of a completely safe self-driving car
- New idea is required as a consequence of a need or a problem in the marketplace
- Because computers can think better and react earlier than people, hence a reliable technology

Award [1] for the correct response and [1] for an explanation. Do not accept if a response is not clear. **[Max 2]**

(b)
- Ergonomically-designed seats
- A smart layout with space for passengers and easy for cleaning and maintenance
- Wide doors which are electrically powered, making it easy for boarding and exiting

- Bright and roomy ambience
- Powerful electric heating, ventilation and air conditioning system for a comfortable journey
- Noise reduction by reducing the stress levels in passengers

Award [1] each for identifying three human factors applied in designing the interiors of the bus. **[Max 3]**

(c)
- System operations
  - Physical access of the passengers. Service visibility to understand how the system works which may include timetables, maps and in-vehicle information sources, capacity of passengers, etc.
- Safety
  - Vehicular, personal
- Comfort
  - Conducive to personal activities of the passengers, pleasing to the senses, clean, spacious, personal space, etc.
- Journey experience
  - Relaxation, attractive, social interaction, convenient, perception of speed/journey time
- Status and image
  - Ownership, environmentally responsible as lower emissions, image of newness, conducive to political support

Award [1] each for identifying the three design criteria and [1] each for an explanation of each design criteria. **[Max 6]**

(d) Growth stage:
- The market has accepted the use of electric/hybrid vehicles as a result of increasing pollution
- This has increased the demand/sales of the electric/hybrid vehicles
- This has also led to increase in many research and development opportunities

Planned obsolescence:
- Designers may limit the effective layout/concept of the electric/hybrid bus
- So as the users can demand or expect new versions of the buses
- This may lead to an increase in the revenue of the country

Further development:
- Designers may integrate better technologies to the next generation of electric/hybrid bus, which may satisfy the need/demand for new features in the bus
- This will also keep the product competitive in the market

Award [2] each for the three correct responses of the electric/hybrid bus relative to its growth, planned obsolescence and further development. And award [1] each for the explanation of each response. **[Max 9]**

7. (a)
- The components can be clearly recognized
- Accessibility to use the components
- Material used is wood, hence can be recycled
- It is a minimalist design as it is comprised of less parts
- No permanent fittings used

Award [1] for each. Do not accept if a response is not clear. **[Max 2]**

(b)
- The wooden planks are under tension as the user will sit on/will apply force to it/weight to it
- The slits provide the wooden planks proper stability
- It prevents the dislocation of the wooden planks from the flexible arrangements
- The thickness of the wooden pieces will resist distortion under tension
- It makes it safe for the user to use

Award [3] for the response with a correct explanation. **[Max 3]**

(c) Anthropometric factors:
- Data related to children's size, weight and age will be considered
- However, the overall size of the chair is fixed
- The chair is manufactured for mass production, so the 50th percentile of size and weight of children will be considered
- Posture and leg space should be accounted so it is comfortable for the user in all the arrangements
- Ensure the tallest and shortest traits of children can use it since it is adjustable

Physiological factors:
- Can be uncomfortable if used for long hours
- The curved shape fits appropriately to the human body while sitting
- Less risk of injuries as no sharp corners and the design is symmetric by nature
- Biomechanical forces are required to make it adjustable for different arrangements

Award [3] for the correct response on applied anthropometrics and [3] on applied physiological factors. **[Max 6]**

(d) • It is flexible so can be used to make the edge curved
- It can be used to form complex shapes
- It can be laminated, adding different variety to the veneers
- High strength-to-weight ratio
- It has good dimensional stability
- It has good mechanical properties which provides good tensile and compressive strength
- It holds good aesthetics and can be finished finely
- It has a good resistance to moist environments
- It maintains its shape, unlike hardwood/softwood which undergoes warping
- Makes the chair durable and long lasting

Award [1] for each of the three features of plywood. And [2] for the explanation of each feature. **[Max 9]**

Set B: Higher Level: Paper 3

Section A

1. (a) • There is a large population problem in most of the developing/developed countries. Roads and highways are congested and there is an increase in the number of car owners. This has led to increased congestion on main roads. PRT may reduce the dependence on individual transport systems
- People travelling in same direction and same time can use PRT and reach destination at the expected time without delay due to congestion
- PRT system uses electricity and so causes less of an environmental impact than cars

Award [1] each for the two reasons of skyTran making public transport system more efficient. **[Max 2]**

(b) • The skyTran is a complex and innovative system which will require diversity in skills, information and viewpoints of experts from various subjects, such as engineers, architects, ethnographers, town planners, designers, IT system specialists, etc.
- Multidisciplinary design teams allow for critical solving of problems due to people having different skills and expertise. Ideas from one person can inspire a different idea for another person. Thus sharing and building on each other's ideas helps to design a more effective solution.
- A multidisciplinary design team provides a deeper understanding of complicated design problems related with user needs. Multiple perspectives involved in the team ensures the study of all possible aspects associated with the designing of the product from manufacturing to its end of life are considered.

Award [1] for the need of a multidisciplinary design team and [1] for its explanation. **[Max 2]**

(c) • Psychologists study human behaviours and emotions to develop a deeper understanding towards their needs and behaviours
  - they can gather data from the point of view of the population or the subject of the study of the system.
- Psychologists understand the value of empathy. While designing systems there is always a gap between humans and the systems designed. Psychologists bridge the gap by empathizing with users.
- They can predict if the PRT would be an accepted solution by the demographics of the country.

Award [1] for the role of a psychologist and [1] for its explanation. **[Max 2]**

(d) • User experience increases product recognition and acceptance, which creates a positive user interaction by reducing the travelling time and by increasing passenger comfort
  - by affording easy accessibility for a varied range of users, the ease of movement within the skyTran will make more

people use it, making the system economical to run and hence can contribute to the success.
- User experience in the computer controllers will reduce errors thus will increase safety
  - this will build user confidence and increases the use of the skyTran system and hence can contribute to the success.
- Absence of the driver or the operator will reduce the overall training costs and the accidents
  - this will eventually lower the cost of operating the skyTran resulting positively on the fare.

Award [1] for each of the two correct reasons for user experience and award [1] for each correct explanation of the reasons. **[Max 4]**

2. (a) • The use of rubber reduces the amount of plastic being used and disposed of
- Toys made from 100% natural material (rubber) can be recycled with appropriate facilities, hence aiding the circular economy
- Encourages public and environment health unlike plastic which is harmful at the end of life
- The sales contribute towards local economy of the forest bearers of the Hevea trees

Award [1] for each way showing the toy as an example of eco design. **[Max 2]**

(b) • The toy provides an alternative to plastic toys
- There is an increase in the number of consumers who are demanding for natural or organic products. The toy only uses natural materials and food-grade paint
  - this allows consumers to make a conscious choice to buy a product that does not harm the environment
- Sophie La Girafe has a responsibility to shareholders to make a profit but its strategies for innovation also focus on improving the lives of poor people in developing countries
- The eco-design strategy is embedded in the design brief for all their products so it promotes ethical consumerism across the total customer base

Award [1] for identifying how the toy can be seen as an example of ethical consumerism and [1] for a brief explanation. **[Max 3]**

(c) • Eco-design is an approach to designing products with special consideration for environmental impacts during its whole life cycle
- It focuses on three broad environmental categories: materials, energy and pollution or waste

Award [2] for the correct response with a brief description. **[Max 2]**

(d) • **Material:** Since it is made from natural material (rubber) it allows for ergonomic shape or form. The latex is soft, elastic, waterproof, insulating and pleasant to smell and touch. The form also allows for stimulating the five senses and is perfect for a baby's small hands.
- **Health:** It is non-toxic, hygienic, provides high-quality health benefits and has compliance from the European and international standards.
- **Usability:** It functions as any other baby-teething toy would. It has the same usability (functionality) as existing toys. It has an ergonomic design which is comfortable for the baby to hold/grip and use from an early age. Balancing all three aspects of the toy has resulted in a functional design and leads to product success in the market. Each of the three aspects are important and are interlinked with each other: if one usability consideration failed, the toy would fail.

Award [1] for any three of the distinct points in an explanation of how the toy balances material, health and usability considerations with a brief description. **[Max 3]**

Section B

3. (a) • Literature research
- Expert appraisal or subject matter expert
- User trial and observations
- User research and questionnaires
- Perceptual mapping
- Environmental scanning

Award [1] for each of the above correct responses. **[Max 3]**

(b) • Involving the users throughout the design process and development.
- Involving users in testing of the designs and in the prototype testing sessions. Also called usability testing sessions

– the modifications are implemented based on users' feedback (design cycle being an iterative process). Award [1] for each of the correct responses for the role of the users. And [1] for a brief explanation. **[Max 2]**

(c) Good understanding of user:
- The designer needs to empathize with the users of the products
- Clear understanding of users' needs, wants and limitations should be researched
- This can be done by involving the users throughout the design and development of the oximeter, which can also be called participatory design as users participate in the design process

Good understanding of task:
- The designer needs to understand how the users will interact with the oximeter.
- The manner of functions the user performs should be understood. This may lead to understanding tasks which users cannot perform easily.
- Through prototype testing, the designer should develop a good understanding of the users' task.

Good understanding of environment:
- The designer should understand where users will use the oximeter
- Through performance testing or field research in appropriate environments, designers can develop a good understanding of the users' environment

Award [1] for any of the above design requirements the designer should understand and award [1] for a brief explanation. **[Max 2]**

(d)
- Learnability is how easy or intuitive it is for a person to learn how to use the oximeter.
- It also means how much help training/support/instructions are given to a person using it.
- The users should be willing to use it with a very little memory burden. Thus giving users a good user experience.
- Positive attitude of users' opinions, feelings and perspectives towards the oximeter.
- Making the design more readable and minimalistic will increase product acceptance and encourages users to buy and recommend others to buy it.

Award [2] for a correct description relating to learnability and [2] for a correct description relating to attitude **[Max 4]**

(e) Socio-pleasure:
- The users will feel more comfortable and so will be more accepted in the society
- A feeling of belonging to a group of people who use oximeters and are not excluded from normal activities
- Status conveyed to others by recommending the oximeter initiates a social conversation

Physio-pleasure:
- By wearing or operating the oximeter
- Pleasure from offering the satisfaction to people suffering from respiratory or cardiovascular problems
- Pleasure from comfortably using the oximeter

Ideo-pleasure:
- The oximeter has good aesthetic and technological value
- Pleasure from feeling normal and less restricted to medical treatments
- It is non-invasive type of service that the device offers

Award [3] for the explanation of each of the socio-pleasures, physio-pleasures and ideo-pleasures. **[Max 9]**

Set C

Standard Level: Paper 1

Question No.	Answer	Question No.	Answer
1	D	16	D
2	C	17	A
3	A	18	D
4	B	19	B
5	C	20	C
6	D	21	C
7	B	22	C

Question No.	Answer	Question No.	Answer
8	D	23	A
9	B	24	B
10	D	25	C
11	A	26	C
12	C	27	A
13	D	28	C
14	A	29	A
15	B	30	B

Higher Level: Paper 1

Question No.	Answer	Question No.	Answer	Question No.	Answer
1	D	16	D	31	B
2	C	17	A	32	C
3	A	18	D	33	A
4	B	19	B	34	C
5	C	20	C	35	D
6	D	21	A	36	C
7	B	22	C	37	B
8	D	23	A	38	C
9	B	24	D	39	C
10	D	25	B	40	D
11	A	26	C		
12	C	27	A		
13	C	28	C		
14	A	29	C		
15	B	30	A		

Set C: Standard and Higher Level: Paper 2

Section A

1 (a) (i) Award [1] for stating a feature and [1] for description:
- S Pen
  – Stylus appeals to visual users who want to draw on their phone
- Bluetooth enabled
  – Allows users to control when the pen becomes a mouse **[Max 2]**

(ii) Award [1] for identifying a reason why water cooling system is and [1] for a brief explanation:
- This prevents the overheating of the phone/reduces phone radiating heat
  – meaning the phone can be used on an activity for a longer duration, such as games, which can have a long playtime **[Max 2]**

(b) (i) Award [1] for identifying an advantage of Bluetooth-enabled technology and [1] for a brief explanation:
- Being Bluetooth enabled means it can be used remotely for useful purposes
  – allowing users to take photos using S Pen button
  – or during a presentation the S Pen can change slides **[Max 2]**

(ii) Award [1] for identifying unique features and [1] for a brief explanation:
- The stylus is a unique feature
  – to appeal to creative and visual people who enjoy making notes or drawings. The stylus can take photos from a distance and also can be used in presentations as a mouse to change slides
- Water-cooling features
  – prolongs phones from overheating **[Max 2]**

(c) (i) Award [1] for each distinct point in a brief explanation:
- Expensive/does it warrant the price and affordability
- Are the enabled features really aimed at specific market segment, e.g. stylus if you don't like visual notes or communication methods **[Max 2]**

(ii) Award [1] for each of the three distinct points in an explanation:
- Using the S Pen feels like pen and paper, for people who think and communicate visually
- Bluetooth-enabled S Pen adds new possibilities, such as acting as mouse in presentation
- HDMI-enabled allows for further presentation adaptations without needing a laptop **[Max 3]**

(d) (i) • One machine
- Combines different feature aspects (such as Bluetooth projector-enabled mouse) **[Max 2]**

(ii) Award [1] for answer identifying why:
- Portability; elements are all integrated to one device

Award [1] for a brief explanation:
- Impact for presentations, easier/quicker to present without switching between devices
- Fewer products/less need to purchase separate products/ save money/save space
- Less materials, energy and resources are used up/more resources are conserved
- Less waste/pollution manufacture **[Max 2]**

(e) (i) Award [1] for identifying each correct mobile phone:
- LG G7 thinQ (lowest)
- HTC Google Pixel (highest) **[Max 2]**

(ii) Award [1] for one factor and [1] for a brief explanation:
- It is in manufacturer's interest to reduce levels of radiation
  - to increase sales from consumers who care about radiation levels
  - because if people get ill from radiation they could sue their manufacturer **[Max 2]**

(iii) Award [1] for one factor and [1] for a brief explanation:
- SAR ratings allows the savvy, interested costumer to consider if a phone emits too much radiation (such phones would appeal to consumers who were concerned about levels of radiation)
  - makes consumers aware of differing radiation levels, within everyday contexts/radiation is quite an abstract consideration for many people **[Max 2]**

(iv) Award [1] for one factor and [1] for a brief explanation:
- SAR is one factor to consider in the design
  - so the designer can make better informed choices in choosing materials which absorb radiation levels **[Max 2]**

2. Award [1] for one factor and [1] for a brief explanation:
- Motion capture software assists with the designer's understanding of human factors, physical limitations of users and product evaluation
  - For example, the user can replay an event in slow motion to analyse a specific focus, such as a car crash or effect of an air pillow **[Max 2]**

3. Award [1] for each point:
- Five-times stronger than steel
- Twice as strong as Kevlar
- Highly elastic
- Waterproof
- Resistant to bacterial breakdown
- Ten times stronger than cellulose and collagen **[Max 3]**

Section B

4. (a) Award [1] for one factor and [1] for a brief explanation:
- Concept model as prototype demonstrates and explains well the principle of a radical new hybrid vehicle
- If sufficient interest, then this would warrant Hyundai moving into a new sector and investing further **[Max 2]**

(b) (i) Award [1] for each factor/explanation:
- Cockpit has exit on each of its four sides
- Allowing easy access to enter/exit the vehicle
- Different walking and speed modes to differentiate terrain conditions
- Increasing comfort for passengers
- Will still function as conventional car
- More convenient for travelling on normal terrain to difficult areas **[Max 3]**

(ii) Award [1] for one factor and [1] for a brief explanation:
- Legs can move in six directions
  - so it can manoeuvre and climb over obstacles
- Legs are retractable/has both legs and wheels
  - means flat or hilly terrain can be traversed
- Legs have two walking modes: reptilian and mammalian
  - meaning it is suitable for rough conditions, such as space or war zones **[Max 3]**

4. (c) (i) Award [1] for each factor/explanation:
- The vehicle could be adopted for military, disaster zones or space missions
- This is another market they are not currently targeting
- Hyundai wants to test the market reaction to see potential **[Max 3]**

(ii) Award [1] for each of three distinct points in relation to the military, space industry and humanitarian organizations [3 max per market, 9 max]

Military
- Can be used in dangerous areas (for example, where there are land mines) as the vehicle can be controlled remotely
- Can traverse obstacles in hostile environments
- More flexible than other military vehicles as it can also be driven in an urban environment on normal roads
- Uses the technology of electric cars so other supplies can be transported instead of fuel

Space industry
- Remotely controlled so it could go on unmanned missions
- The legs allow the vehicle to climb over hazardous, uneven terrain
- Future-orientated design would be appealing to the space industry
- Uses the technology of electric cars so no other dangerous fuel needs to be transported in space

Humanitarian organizations
- The cockpit specifically has four-door access which could be important in humanitarian rescue situations
- The electric actuator technology enables Elevate to climb over walls up to 5 foot high which could help in natural disaster zones such as earthquakes
- Passengers are kept level which would benefit injured passengers in a rescue
- (As with military) uses the technology of electric cars so other supplies can be transported instead of fuel. **[Max 9]**

5. (a) (i) Award [1] for one factor and [1] for a brief explanation:
- The wingsuit has been purposefully designed to allow a human to glide through the air
- Wingsuiting is a sport in its own right/the wingsuit would have no use other than for wingsuiting
- The design of the wingsuit is vital for the performance and health and safety of the user **[Max 2]**

(ii) Award [1] for one factor and [1] for a brief explanation:
- Ripstop nylon, as found in parachutes:
  - necessitating flight to remain airborne
  - allowing user to perform different motions: free fall, stunts, glide, navigation
  - the material compensating wind resistant, g-force from extreme elements, such as sun, rain, hail, strong winds **[Max 2]**

(b) (i) Award [1] for one factor and [1] for a brief explanation:
- The suit is symmetrical, so the steering is not affected while wingsuiting
- The suit is well stitched, so that no tears or splits occur **[Max 2]**

(ii) Award [1] for one factor and [1] for a brief explanation:
- Whalebone would be used to make airfoil
  - because it is strong to withstand wind resistance **[Max 2]**

(iii) Award [1] for each factor/explanation:
- Airfoil is created from ripstop nylon material with specific designated folds, which are sewn together
- It works by utilizing the resistance of the air: air is pushed through inlets in the suit to inflate membranes, which helps maintain the airfoil as semirigid **[Max 3]**

(c) Award [1] for each of three distinct points in relation to usefulness, effectiveness and learnability. [3 max per aspect, 9 max].

Usefulness
- The wing system allows the user to easily glide so they can perform somersaults, do complex manoeuvres and steer accurately
- Works with minimal effort required by the user
- Adapts to different climatic conditions for comfort of user

Effectiveness
- Users can vary speed and are in control: can thrust up or down and change direction
- The unique 'skin', layering of the fabric, whether single suit or individual sections determines the effectiveness, efficiency and performance
- The texture and layering of fabric is comfortable for users
- Three individual ram-air wings are attached: between the legs, one under each arm, utilizes air resistance, where air is pushed through inlets in the suit to inflate membranes – helps maintain the airfoil as semirigid

Learnability
- Intuitive – easy to use without any specialist training or guidance
- It facilitates the user in free fall by being able to adjust intuitively.
- Memorable for regular users to use without relearning **[Max 9]**

6. (a) Award [1] for one factor and [1] for a brief explanation:
- Dome roof, 6 glass panels, cast iron, signage illuminate, crown crest **[Max 2]**

(b) Award [1] for one factor and [1] for a brief explanation:
- The fact that this comes in four sections allows portability and manoeuvrability
- Can be delivered, assembled and bolted on site **[Max 2]**

(c) Award [1] for each point:
- Cast iron can be manufactured by each section being cast from male mould
- Could be fabricated in wood (such as plywood)
- The concrete base could again be precast
- Using wooded shuttering (such as plywood)
- These at the time were mass produced, using assembly method **[Max 4]**

(d) Award [1] for one factor and [1] for a brief explanation:
- Teak, being a hardwood, has strong characteristics and can withstand harsh weather, such as rain and sun
- The door needs to fit the box so it is important the wood does not shrink or warp...
- ... and teak properties are resistant to this compared to many other woods **[Max 3]**

(e) Award [1] for each of three distinct points. [3 max for each separate explanation].

Image
The distinct colour red makes it stand out / its design makes it instantly recognisable / it creates an emotional or nostalgic response

Form
Unique geometrical classical shape / memorable features (e.g. font, crown design) / crown design/royal crest very British to have local and international appeal

Function
It's humanistic in terms of human factors and well ergonomically designed (e.g. ventilation) / it is user friendly (e.g. a wheelchair user can fit in) / comfortable to use (e.g. the way the teak door opens and closes softly) / the small windows gives it light but still provides privacy to the user when making a phone call

Mass production
The cast-iron structure means it can be transported and efficiently erected on site / ability to mass produce means many could be quickly and they became a common feature

Timeless appeal
The product is a standard product of its time / it has enduring popularity and iconic status globally / it is clearly a product of a specific time **[Max 9]**

Set C: Paper 3

Section A

1. (a) Accept any two responses. Award [1] for each correct response and [1] for an explanation. Accept any other reasonable suggestion.
- Motion sensor
- Directly in tune with user gestures
- One-hand operational
- Rings means it becomes wearable **[Max 4]**

(b) Award [1] for identifying a reason and [1] for a brief explanation:
- Time to learn and master new ways of operation
- Price
- A completely different system is intimidating **[Max 2]**

(c) Award [1] for each of the three distinct points in an explanation of the implications of Shape Product designs for the user and [1] for each separate and distinct explanation:
- Bluetooth-enabled
  - users can use TAP keyboard/mouse designers readily with other Bluetooth-enabled devices
- The TAP keyboard/mouse designers has been sustainably designed
  - so it is easy and economical to recycle
- Compatible with TAP Genius app
  - user-friendly and self-supporting app **[Max 6]**

2. (a) Award [1] for each benefit listed of the Yamaha company creating a distinctive brand identity.
- Continual incremental improvement
- Workers employ analytical techniques such as value stream mapping
- 5 whys to quickly identify opportunities, eliminate waste and improve productivity **[Max 2]**

(b) Award [1] for identifying a reason why the Yamaha company would use market segmentation as part of its product development strategy and [1] for a brief explanation:
- Economic viability, during this time an economic downturn, i.e. cash tight for many householders
- Cost effectiveness, marketing, transportation, etc.
- Mood not of optimism, but that of constraint and frugality. This costs more than a 2-wheeler scooter **[Max 3]**

(c) Award [1] for identifying a reason of how CIM can lead to Yamaha's greater efficiency and [1] for a brief explanation:
- CIM to increase productivity
  - meaning there is the potential for cost savings
- CIM links design, engineering, manufacturing and industrial robots via automation
  - therefore synchronising four distinctive areas
- Monitors and controls operations from raw materials throughout production process
  - more consistent and does not need a break like a human worker **[Max 3]**

Section B

3. (a) Award [1] for a benefit listed of merger on this project of Airbus and Audi company and [1] for brief explanation:
- By combining forces, through alliance, both Airbus and Audi are pioneering
- They are charting a new and innovative course
- Airbus and Audi show willingness for product diversification **[Max 2]**

(b) Award [1] for stating a new technological area:
- Drones, electric, autonomous flying cars are all relatively new areas
- Combining hybrid approach and fusion of so many new advances into one product
- In some ways, similar to a transformer, in terms of various multi-functional usage **[Max 1]**

(c) Award [1] for identifying a reason how Airbus and Audi enhance their branding and [1] for a brief explanation:
- Both Airbus and Audi's reputations are enhanced, as electric and autonomous flying cars are currently popular and so will be reported in the media

- By association to these relatively hot emerging areas, Airbus and Audi become synonymous with latest technology and innovation
- Both companies show they are interested in pioneering

[Max 2]

(d) Award [1] for identifying each point and [1] for a brief explanation per point:
  - Hybrid approach
  - Innovative as it combines autonomy, drones and electricity in cars
  - Acts as transformer, combining different innovative solutions
    – to perform different functions and tasks, as required
  - Pioneering in sense venturing into new ground
    – using autonomous drones, with electric specifically   **[Max 6]**

(e) Award [1] for identifying a reason [1 to 2] for a brief explanation per point:
  - Appearance at Turin Motor Show
    – identifies with current areas of high interest
    – i.e. autonomous, electric self-driving cars and passenger drones
  - For Audi, Airbus and Italdesign, the prototype is an important milestone in transportation technology
    – providing a collaboration and convergence
  - Amsterdam Drone week
    – connects with drones, which now are directly merging themselves, and closely resembling helicopters, as passenger drones becomes more prevalent
    – at the same time, by also exhibiting in the Turin Motor Show, it still conforms to a status of being perceived as a car, which reflects Audi's vision
  - Scale-model prototype as a live demo allows people to see, visualize and experience it in person
  - It allows people to be able to see different intended contexts, to weigh up scope and significance
    – some people consider this flying drone as the future of taxis (pioneering)
  - This vehicle could transcend future trends in cities in terms of reducing traffic and congestion   **[Max 9]**

Printed in Australia
AUHW010532021019
318059AU00003B/22